Study Guide

for

CONTEMPORARY SOCIETY
An Introduction to Social Science

Study Guide

for

CONTEMPORARY SOCIETY
An Introduction to Social Science
Ninth Edition

JOHN A. PERRY
Cuyahoga Community College

ERNA K. PERRY

Allyn and Bacon
Boston   London   Toronto   Sydney   Tokyo   Singapore

ISBN 0-205-31772-3

Printed in the United States of America

10 9 8 7 6 5 4 3 2 1   03 02 01 00 99

TABLE OF CONTENTS

CHAPTER 1

THROUGH THE LENS OF SCIENCE

In this chapter, you will learn

1. of the existence of the external, physical world, which we inherit, and the social world, which we create;
2. that the analysis of the social world with the tools of science is a fairly recent innovation;
3. the basic differences between the social and the natural sciences;
4. the elements and steps of the scientific method;
5. which disciplines constitute the social sciences;
6. the various research methods used in the social sciences.

TOPICAL OUTLINE

I. SCIENCE LOOKS AT SOCIETY
    A. The Social Sciences and the Physical Sciences Differentiated
    B. The Social World Through the Lens of Science
        1. Concepts
        2. Theories
        3. Research
            a. Variables: Independent and Dependent
    C. The Scientific Method
        1. Steps of the Scientific Method
            a. Selecting and defining a topic
            b. Developing a Research Design
            c. Verifying
            d. Generalizing
    D. The Scientific Spirit: Skepticism, Objectivity, Relativity

II. THE SOCIAL SCIENCE DISCIPLINES
    A. Anthropology
    B. Economics
    C. Geography
        1. Demography
        2. Ecology
    D. History
    E. Political Science
    F. Psychology
    G. Sociology

III. RESEARCH METHODS IN THE SOCIAL SCIENCES
   A. Sample Survey
   B. Case Studies
   C. Participant Observation
   D. Experiment
   E. Statistical Analysis
      1. Central Tendency
      2. Mean
      3. Median

A. CHAPTER OVERVIEW

The social sciences are concerned with the **social universe** which is the creation of people and results from their group way of life. Unfortunately, this social universe is difficult to analyze dispassionately and **objectively** because it involves people studying people. The **physical** sciences are more **advanced** than the social sciences because physical scientists do not let **emotion** color their research. Humans, however, cannot be studied with the same methods as inanimate objects or other animals because they cannot help but develop relationships with the subjects of their analysis.

A. FILL IN THE BLANKS:

1. The social sciences are concerned with the ___Social Universe___ which is a creation of people.
2. _____ is a problem in the social sciences.
3. Physical scientists can be more _advanced_ and less _emotion_ than social scientists.
4. Humans tend to develop _relationship_ with the subjects they analyze.
5. Humans cannot be studied with the methods of the _inanimate objects_.

B. CHAPTER OVERVIEW

The scientific method is an integral part of science and its use confers the term "science" upon any subject. The scientific method consists of a series of steps. First, the area of research must be **selected**. Second, the problem to be researched must be clearly **stated** and **defined**. Then, a **hypothesis** should be formulated. (A hypothesis is a statement of the problem and its possible solution.) The problem under investigation must then be carefully **observed**, **described**, and **recorded**. The observed data are further classified and organized to show whether there are patterns and relationships. From the above steps it is possible to **generalize** about the subject being researched. This generalization will either **validate**, **reform**, or **contradict** the hypothesis with which the researcher began research. The generalization, if the research is successfully replicated, may become a scientific **theory**. On rare occasions, if the theory explains all phenomena to which it is applied, it becomes a scientific **law**. But neither theories nor laws remain unchallenged. They are always undergoing **changes** and **revisions**.

B. FILL IN THE BLANKS:

1. A _hypothesis_ is a general statement of the problem at hand and its possible solution.
2. _____ _____ refers to the use of human senses and precision instruments to study the subject under consideration in all its aspects.
3. Emerging patterns and relationships are shown through _whether_ _organized_ and _recorded_ .
4. A formal description of the behavior of certain phenomena under specific conditions is called _Law_ .

C. CHAPTER OVERVIEW

The social sciences include: **anthropology**, divided into **physical** anthropology, concerned with human biological origins and variation and drawing upon the natural sciences, and **cultural** anthropology dealing with preliterate societies or subgroups in their cultural variation (**archaeology** is yet another subfield of anthropology concerning itself with past societies that did not leave a written record); **sociology**, focusing on group dynamics and the forces at work when humans interact, with a stress on contemporary and mainly Western societies; **psychology**, analyzing the forces that shape and motivate individuals; **economics**, attempting to understand how societies solve the universal problem of scarcity and thus dealing with processes of supply and demand, markets, money, trade, regulation, work, etc.; **political science**, concerned with the need for government, its form, and its processes, as well as with the behavior of individuals in the political arena; **history**, which is not always studied with the scientific method, but when it is, it provides a context in which to study human relationships, as well as a sequence of related events, systematically.

Geography, which is a natural science, has features of a social science when it concerns itself with the behavior of people in a specific environment and the ways in which they use the natural environment. **Demography** (the study of population) and **ecology** (the study of the relationships between all living organisms and their natural environment) are part of geography. Even **genetics**, the science of heredity, has become important to social scientists as they try to learn about human behavior.

All of the social sciences are **interrelated** in that they all revolve around the behavior of people in social settings. The various disciplines emerged when vast amounts of information began to accumulate so rapidly that **specialization** became necessary.

C. FILL IN THE BLANKS:

1. The social science discipline that is a combination of a natural and a social science is ___Geography___.

2. ___Archaeology___ is a field of anthropology which concerns itself with historical data about past societies without a written record.

3. An emphasis on contemporary, mainly Western societies, is a feature of ___Sociology___.

4. In tracing the development of the newborn infant into a functioning member of society we draw upon the knowledge of the discipline of _____.

5. Supply and demand, the production, distribution, and consumption of goods and services, the value of work and of natural resources are all factors examined by the discipline of _____.

6. Concepts such as the state, power, ideology and their effects on the behavior of individuals are analyzed in the context of _____ _____.

7. History is not universally considered a _____ _____.

D. CHAPTER OVERVIEW

Social scientists use such methods as **field observation** aided by **statistical data**, in-depth personal **interviews**, **case studies**, and **participant observation**. They also use **sampling techniques**, a method in which a small number of respondents represents a large population fairly accurately; **statistical correlation**, in which relationships between two or more sets of data can be established; and **probability statistics**, through which the likelihood of a result having occurred by chance can be measured. **Statistical analysis** includes descriptive statistics (mean, median, mode) which convey the central tendency--what is typical--of a group of numbers, and inferential statistics which provide the techniques researchers use to decide if they can make valid statements about a specific population based on a particular sample of it. In addition, investigators may use **in-depth analysis techniques**, detailed **personal** histories in which emotions may surface; **experiments** in which researchers interfere with natural conditions in order to find out how individuals respond in specific situations; and **simulation** models. And much of social science remains **descriptive** and cannot be definitively tested.

searchers depended to a large degree on statistical and **quantita-** investigating human behavior, observing and describing social making judgments about it. Most social scientists today realize that **total objectivity** is impossible; however, they attempt to attain as much objectivity as they can.

D. FILL IN THE BLANKS:

1. Relationships between two or among more sets of data can be easily summarized through _____.
2. The likelihood that a certain result occurs by chance is measured by _probability_ _statistics_ .
3. _____ _____ allow a small number of respondents to represent fairly accurately large populations.
4. In the past, social scientists were expected to refrain from making _quantitative_ about social reality.

TERMS TO REMEMBER

case study: A method of research consisting of a detailed, long-term investigation of a single social unit.

concept: A generalized idea about people, objects, or processes that are related to one another; an abstract way of classifying things that are similar.

ethical neutrality: An attitude of the scientific method in the social sciences, requiring that scientists not pass moral judgment on their findings.

experiment: A method of research in which the researcher controls and manipulates variables in one group in order to test the effects of an independent variable on a dependent variable.

hypothesis: A tentative statement, in clearly defined terms, predicting a relationship between variables.

objectivity: A principle of the scientific method, especially in the social sciences, requiring researchers to divest themselves of personal attitudes, desires, beliefs, values, and tendencies when confronting their data.

participant observation: A method of research in which researchers try to take part in the lives of the members of the group under analysis, sometimes without revealing their purposes.

research: An aspect of scientific methodology that bolsters and complements theories. In the social sciences, four fundamental formats are used: the sample survey, the case study, the experiment, and participant observation.

5

sample survey: A method of research consisting of an attempt to determine the occurrence of a particular act or opinion in a particular sample of people.

theory: A set of concepts arranged so as to explain and/or predict possible and probable relationships.

variables: Factors whose relationships researchers try to uncover; characteristics that differ (vary) in each individual case, as opposed as to the constant, a characteristic that remains the same.

HOW MUCH DO YOU RECALL? TEST YOUR KNOWLEDGE

MULTIPLE CHOICE QUESTIONS

1.   Humans are born into:
      a. a social world based on instincts
      b. environments with no pasts
      c. social worlds with traditions
      d. physical worlds created by preceding generations

2.   The social sciences use methods based on:
      a. speculation
      b. artistic insights
      c. philosophies of life
      d. none of the above

3.   The scientific method is based on:
      a. verification of evidence
      b. replication of scientific investigation
      c. objectivity
      d. all of the above

4.   Which is not a step of the scientific method?
      a. intuition
      b hypothesis
      c. observation and recording
      d. generalization

5.   Which is not a characteristic of science?
      a. logical
      b. propositional
      c. authoritarian
      d. public

6. Science offers explanations for observations that are inexplicable by the senses alone; therefore, it is:
    a. empirical
    b. continuous
    c. self-correcting
    d. problem solving

7. The classification and organization of data:
    a. are the first step in the scientific method
    b. are called empirical research
    c. are vital because they show emerging patterns
    d. tell the scientist if a hypothesis is correct

8. Which is not exclusively a social science?
    a. geography
    b. history
    c. archaeology
    d. all of the above

9. It is easier to study physical phenomena because:
    a. they are concrete
    b. it is easier to be objective
    c. the researchers belong to the same species
    d. they are closer to the investigator

10. Which is not a method of social science research:
    a. vivisection
    b. case study
    c. sample survey
    d. participant observation

11. The Industrial Revolution brought about:
    a. the development of two new classes
    b. the migration of job seekers to cities
    c. the emergence of social sciences
    d. all of the above

12. Which is <u>not</u> a characteristic of scientific theory? It:
    a. explains and predicts
    b. has the force of a law
    c. is open to challenge by scientific evidence
    d. is founded on observations, concepts, and analysis

13. Scientific explanations are superior to common sense be   cause:

a. they are always subject to revision
b. they are made by trained observers
c. scientific observation is systematic and precise
d. all of the above

14. Experiments:
    a. are always conducted in experimental labs
    b. are used exclusively by psychologists
    c. involve keeping all variables constant except one
    d. permit study of group culture from the inside

15. History is not entirely a social science because:
    a. historians refuse to be scientific
    b. historians study meaningful relationships
    c. history's primary object is to record human events
    d. social science is primarily concerned with the present

ANSWERS

ANSWERS TO FILL IN THE BLANKS:

A. 1. social universe
    2. objectivity
    3. objective, emotional
    4. relationships
    5. physical sciences

B. 1. hypothesis
    2. Empirical research
    3. classification and organization

C. 1. anthropology
    2. Archaeology
    3. sociology
    4. psychology
    5. economics
    6. political science
    7. social science

D. 1. statistical correlation
    2. probability statistics
    3. sampling techniques

4. judgment

ANSWERS TO MULTIPLE CHOICE QUESTIONS

1. c	6. a	11. d
2. d	7. c	12. b
3. d	8. d	13. d
4. a	9. b	14. c
5. c	10. a	15. c

CHAPTER 2

IN THE BEGINNING...

In this chapter, you will learn

1. of the theories concerning the origin of the universe within which the planet Earth exists;
2. how life on earth began, according to the latest research findings;
3. the basic concepts, including the processes of natural selection, that comprise the theory of evolution;
4. the importance and the basic principles of genetics;
5. the historical stages of human evolution as shown by the fossil record;
6. the appearance of agriculture and its consequences;
7. the biological foundations of human culture.

TOPICAL OUTLINE

I. THE UNIVERSE
    A. Theories of How it Began
    B. The Earth and the Solar System

II. THE BEGINNINGS OF LIFE
    A. The Emergence of the Theory of Evolution
    B. A Revolution in Thought: Darwin and His Theory
    C. Natural Selection
        1. The Role of Heredity

III. GENETICS
    A. Population Genetics: Factors for Change
        1. Mutation
        2. Genetic Drift
        3. Gene Flow
        4. Speciation
        5. Natural Selection and Adaptation

IV. THE LONG TREK: HUMAN EVOLUTION
    A. From Ape to Hominid
    B. Split Between Chimpanzee and Human Lines
    B. The Road to Homo Sapiens

V. HOMO SAPIENS: MODERN HUMANS

VI. AGRICULTURE: CULTIVATION AND DOMESTICATION

VII. THE EVOLUTION OF HUMAN NATURE
    A. Biological Foundations

A. CHAPTER OVERVIEW

The universe is thought to be between 8 and 12 billion years old. According to the currently dominant theory, the **big bang** theory, it began with a gigantic explosion that was the result of a submicroscopic, infinitely dense and unimaginably hot knot of pure energy that flew outward in all directions, eventually giving rise to radiation and matter. The force of gravity then drew the matter to denser regions which, over billions of years, became galaxies, stars, planets, and everything that exists in the universe.

Microbiologists are concluding that the ultimate ancestors of all living creatures are organisms that still exist in the hottest environments on earth, such as hot springs, geysers, and volcanic vents beneath the sea. These microscopic organisms are called thermophiles, a Greek term meaning "heat loving." Later, simple one-celled organisms developed and acquired the ability to reproduce in the oceans. Growing in complexity, these organisms eventually gave rise to plants and animals. When plants could survive on dry land, the environment was ready to house living things such as huge reptiles, flying birds, and small mammals. Mammals were the most insignificant of the animals, but they were adaptable and survived great climatic changes.

One order of mammals, the primates, took to a life in the trees of the thick forests that were covering the earth and began an evolutionary process that culminated in the emergence of humans.

A. FILL IN THE BLANKS:

1. The "big bang" with which the universe began is said to have occurred
    _____to____ _____years ago.
2. Galaxies and planets were formed because of _____.
3. The universe continues to _____.
4. Most of the universe consists of_____ _____.
5. The earth is probably __ _____years old.
6. In about 1.5 billion years, the sun will become _____and _____the earth.
7. Life began in the form of heat-loving _____and later in the _____.
8. The organisms that fed on plants evolved into _____.

B. CHAPTER OVERVIEW

The line of development of all living creatures from one-celled microorganisms to complex beings such as modern humans is explained by the theory of **evolution**. The idea on which this theory is based--that **species** undergo **changes** to **adapt** to different environments--was not new. It was not generally accepted because it went against the biblical explanation of creation according to which God had created a rigid hierarchy of essentially unchangeable species. The **nineteenth century**, in which many **social and cultural changes** occurred, predisposed scientists to accept the notion of change in animal species, bolstered further by the discoveries of fossils of creatures that were no longer in existence. The **theory of evolution**, proposed by Charles Darwin in his The Origin of the Species, posited that **species are not unchangeable**; that species belonging to the same category are **lineal descendants** of some other species that are probably extinct; and that the **mechanism** of evolutionary change is natural selection. **Natural selection** is a process in which some individuals out of a varied population are, by chance, born with traits that help them survive in a specific environment. They **pass** these traits on to some of their descendants who also flourish, **reproduce**, and transmit the successful trait. The individuals who do not possess such a trait are **less successful**, tend not to live long enough to reproduce, and thus they eventually **disappear** from the population. As the environment changes, or as individuals wander into a new environment, new traits become **adaptive** (leading to success in survival), and the process repeats itself.

The theory of evolution was further **clarified** by the work of **Gregor Mendel** who concluded that traits of two individuals who mate are **not blended**; rather, some traits are **dominant** and tend to appear in the offspring, and others are **recessive** and tend to remain hidden, although they do not disappear completely (they may reappear in future generations when two individuals with the same recessive trait mate). Even minute changes leading to an improvement in the ability to survive could, given sufficient time, result in substantial evolutionary change.

B. FILL IN THE BLANKS:

1. The theory of evolution is based on the notion that species are

_____.

2. In the biblical account of creation, God created an immutable
_____of species

3. A more receptive attitude toward change became evident in the
_____century.

4. Fossils of creatures that were _____were being discovered.

5. The Origin of the Species is the revolutionary work of _____

_____.

6. Evolutionary change occurs through _____ _____.

7. Individuals who lack a trait helpful to survival in a given environment eventually become _____.

8. According to Gregor Mandel, some traits are _____ and others _____.

C. CHAPTER OVERVIEW

Evolution has been bolstered by the science that studies heredity, **genetics**, which is divided into such subfields as chromosomal, biochemical, and population genetics. According to genetics, traits are transmitted by hereditary units called **genes** which contain a blueprint with instructions for the structure of every part of every living organism. Genes are **arranged in linear order** into units called **chromosomes** which are **located** in the **nucleus** of every cell of an organism. Humans have **46 chromosomes**, one-half inherited from each parent. An individual's **genotype** consists of all the hereditary factors contained in his/her genes. An individual's **phenotype** is made up of the visible, or expressed, traits. The genes themselves are made up of a complex biochemical substance called **DNA** which is the basic building block of life. Evolutionary change occurs through mutation, genetic drift, gene flow, and speciation. **Mutations** are permanent changes in genetic material; they are random and on the whole negative. **Genetic drift** occurs when a trait becomes dominant in a segment of the population because of its isolation. **Gene flow** is the movement of genes from one population to another through interbreeding. **Speciation** is the development of a new species as a result of such profound genetic changes that breeding with the original species becomes impossible. Speciation is irreversible.

C. FILL IN THE BLANKS:

1. The science that explores the mechanisms of heredity is _____.
2. Traits are transmitted by _____.
3. Genes are hereditary units containing a _____with instructions for every part of an organism.
4. Genes are arranged in a line into _____.
5. Humans have ____chromosomes located in the _____of every cell.
6. Each parent contributes ____chromosomes to the offspring.
7. All the hereditary factors contained in an individual's genes are his/her _____.
8. A phenotype consists of all the _____, _____, traits.
9. The basic building block of life is called _____.
10. Evolutionary change occurs through _____,_____ _____,_____ _____, and _____.
11. The development of a new species is called _____.
12. Genetic drift occurs when a segment of a population becomes_____.

D. CHAPTER OVERVIEW

One order of **mammals**, the **primates**, began living in trees some 65 million years ago when the earth was covered by forests. Eventually, these primates, called prosimians (ape-like) by anthropologists, developed a fine **grasping mechanism** consisting of hands with fingers and an opposing thumb to hold unto branches; **eyes** in the front of the head for better vision; and a complex **cerebral cortex** to coordinate behavior. About 35 million years ago the prosimians diversified into monkeys and a little later into apes. Some of these apes eventually attempted to live on the ground.

The evolution of modern humans did **not** occur in a **straight line**; rather, more than one group of hominids existed side by side. But, approximately one million years ago only one hominid group remained, called <u>Homo erectus</u> (the upright human), the ancestor of our own species, <u>Homo sapiens</u> (the wise human). Definite <u>Homo sapiens</u> fossils date back 75,000 years ago. Among them are those of the **Neanderthals** who provided the stereotype of the "caveman," and the **Cro-Magnon**, dating from between 30,000 to 35,000 years ago, who belonged to the same species modern humans do. These humans survived primarily through **hunting and gathering** until the invention of agriculture.

Agriculture first appeared in the Near East in an area bordering the Persian Gulf, spread to southeastern Europe about 8000 years ago, and northward and westward for the next 15 to 20 centuries. It brought with it **permanent settlements**, **cities**, and the **domestication of animals**. It also led to surpluses, warfare, and great **population growth**.

D. FILL IN THE BLANKS

1. Extinction is the result of a failure to _____.
2. Mammals originated about _____million years ago.
3. Primates are an order of _____.
4. Life in the trees forced the prosimians to develop a_____, better _____, and a complex_____ _____.
5. The prosimians are the predecessors of _____and _____.
6. Several groups of hominids lived _____.
7. Homo erectus is a precursor of _____ _____.
8. Fossils dating back 30,000 to 35,000 years are attributed to the
_____.
9. Agriculture first appeared in an area called the _____ _____in the
_____ _____.

E. CHAPTER OVERVIEW

At the same time that humans were **evolving biologically**, they were also developing **customs and habits** that helped them survive in their environment, and that differentiated them from other animals. It is important to remember that biological realities have **social consequences**. Thus, humans probably began walking on two feet (bipedalism) for a number of reasons, at first probably only because it helped them see as they walked in the tall grass. But the fact that they **walked on two feet** had a number of very important **social results**: the use of their hands enabled them to carry food from place to place and to manipulate objects with tools.

These tasks made them more intelligent, enlarging their brain. **Large-brained infants** must be born small and immature in order to pass through the mother's birth canal. Such infants require a long period of care and are **dependent on an adult**. A mother caring for a dependent infant is not an effective provider; thus, she may have sought the **protection of a male**, leading to a rudimentary **family bond**. Other **social processes** emerged from the mechanisms of **biological adaptation** among which were probably **cooperation** and sharing, the **incest taboo**, a simple **moral system**, as well as such feelings as gratitude, sympathy, friendship, guilt, shame, and moral indignation.

When groups of humans had grown large in size and complexity, a certain degree of **organization** became necessary. Thus, the emergence of **troops** with leaders and hierarchies of dominance, and eventually **tribes** and tribal unions with an ever-increasing number of rules and procedures.

Progress in the development of **social systems** was much enhanced by the discovery and subordination of fire, which allowed humans to wander much farther into colder climates; to protect themselves from predators; and to live in caves. Indirectly, fire also contributed to **reshaping** the contours of the human face, to increasing the **complexity** of language, to producing feelings of **community**, and to the emergence of **religion**. In short, what we call "human nature," as well as "culture," or the way of life of people, were developing alongside human biological evolution.

E. FILL IN THE BLANKS:

1. Biological realities have _____ consequences.
2. Dependent infants force their mothers to become dependent on _____.
3. Some of the social processes that emerged from the biological change to bipedalism were _____, _____, and _____.
4. When groups of humans grew large they had to submit to various levels of
_____.

5. Living in colder climates and in caves, defending themselves from predators, and eating cooked food followed the discovery of _____.

TERMS TO REMEMBER:

australopithecus: The fossil remains of a prehuman who lived from abound 5 million to 1.5 million years ago. Some researchers maintain that this type of prehuman is not a direct ancestor of modern humans but rather is a contemporary of an upright-walking, meat-eating, large-brained species that survived; others insist that Australopithecus is on the human ancestral line.

chromosomes: Carriers of genes, or the hereditary blueprints of organisms. Each human inherits a set of 23 chromosomes from each parent.

cro-magnon: Fossil remains of the closest predecessors of modern humans who lived about 35,000 years ago. They were expert tool makers and artists and lived in tribes that displayed evidence of rules and kinship systems.

dna: Deoxyribonucleic acid. A complex biochemical substance (protein) that is the basic building block of life. It determines the inheritance of specific traits.

estrus: Period of sexual receptivity and ability to conceive.

evolution: A theory that explains change in living organisms and variation within species. Evolution functions according to
processes of natural selection, mutation, genetic drift, gene flow and speciation.

gene flow: The movement of genes from one gene pool to another. It results in new combinations of genes in the offspring.

gene frequency: The proportion in which the various genes occur in an inbreeding population.

gene pool: All of the genetic material available to a population to be inherited by the next generation.

genes: Hereditary units that transmit an individual's traits. They are contained in the chromosomes and made up of DNA.

genetic drift: The fluctuations in frequencies of specific traits in a small, isolated population, so that visible differences between an isolated population and the population from which it broke away become obvious.

genetics: The science of heredity.

hominids: Prehuman creatures who walked on two feet.

homo erectus: The upright hominid thought to be a direct ancestor of modern humans.

homo sapiens: A species whose fossils date back 75,000 years and include Neanderthal. The species label for modern humans is Homo sapiens sapiens, whose fossils date back 30,000 years and include Cro-Magnon.

mutation: A permanent change in genetic material.

natural selection: A process of evolution in which random traits are tested for their survival value; the successful traits are passed on, while organisms possessing less successful traits eventually become extinct.

neanderthal: A subspecies of Homo sapiens whose fossil remains date from 70,000 to 35,000 years ago. They are known to have buried their dead.

primates: An order of mammals to which monkeys, apes, and humans belong.

ramapithecus: A hominoid having hominid-like features, dated between 8 and 14 million years ago.

HOW MUCH DO YOU RECALL? TEST YOUR KNOWLEDGE

MULTIPLE CHOICE QUESTIONS

1.　According to the "big bang" theory, the universe:
   a. began with a hot knot of pure energy
   b. continues to expand
   c. is between 8 and 12 billion years old
   d. all of the above

2.　Life originated:
   a. in the Far East
   b. in geysers and hot places, and oceans
   c. on dry land
   d. in the atmosphere

3.　Prosimians:
   a. were the ancestors of monkeys, apes, and humans

b. were mammals
c. took to life in trees
d. all of the above

4. Hominids are primates that have:
   a. locomotion on two feet
   b. comparatively large brains
   c. non-protruding faces
   d. all of the above

5. According to anthropologists:
   a. more than one group of hominids lived side by side
   b. humans evolved in a straight line of development
   c. hominids are the ancestors of contemporary apes
   d. humans are descended from the great apes of Africa

6. Along with biological changes, social processes like the following were also emerging:
   a. monogamy
   b. cooperation and sharing
   c. bipedalism
   d. larger brains

7. Which was **not** a result of the discovery of fire?
   a. a new shape for the human face
   b. progress in the development of language and religion
   c. ability to wander further into colder climates
   d. hunting and gathering

8. According to Charles Darwin, the primary mechanism of evolutionary change is:
   a. cross breeding
   b. natural selection
   c. hybridization
   d. phenotype

9. The hereditary units that transmit traits and characteristics are called:
   a. DNA
   b. genotypes
   c. phenotypes
   d. genes

10. Differences among racial groups include:

a. variation in blood type
b. biochemical factors
c. cultural factors
d. only a and b

11. Genetics is concerned with:
    a. how chromosomes transmit genes across generations
    b. the reasons for genetic variations and changes in populations
    c. biochemical and cellular events
    d. all of the above

12. Genetic flow entails:
    a. permanent change in genetic material
    b. the movement of genes from one breeding population to another
    c. the evolution of one species into another
    d. all of the above

13 The loss of estrus in human females:
    a. lessened competition among males for females
    b. built stronger bonds between specific males and females
    c. provided children with two protective adults
    d. all of the above

ANSWERS TO FILL IN THE BLANKS:

A. 1. 8 -12 billion
    2. gravity
    3. expand
    4. dark matter
    5. 5 billion
    6. hotter, melt
    7. one-celled microorganisms, oceans
    9. Animals

B. 1. changeable
    2. hierarchy
    3. l9th
    4. extinct
    5. Charles Darwin
    6. natural selection
    7. extinct
    8. dominant, recessive

C. 1. genetics
    2. genes
    3. blueprint
    4. chromosomes
    5. 46, nucleus
    6. 23
    7. genotype
    8. visible traits
    10. DNA
    11. mutation, genetic drift, gene flow, and speciation
    12. speciation
    13. isolated

D. 1. Reproduce
    2. 65 million
    3. mammals
    4. grasping mechanism, vision, cerebral cortex
    5. monkeys, apes
    6. side by side
    7. homo sapiens
    8. Cro_magnon
    9. Ferticle Crescent, Middle East

E. 1. Social
    2. partners (males)
    3. cooperation, incest taboo, moral system
    4. organization
    5. fire

ANSWERS TO MULTIPLE CHOICE QUESTIONS

1. d
2. b
3. d
4. a
5. a
6. b
7. d
8. b
9. d
10. d
11. d
12. b
13. d

CHAPTER 3

CULTURE: PRODUCT AND GUIDE TO LIFE IN SOCIETY

In this chapter, you will learn

1.   why humans are unique;
2.   the importance of symbols;
3.   the importance of shared meanings;
4.   why culture is responsible for all human progress and the evolution of societies;
5.   what culture consists of;
6.   why norms are vital to societies;
7.   the difference between the attitudes of ethnocentrism and cultural relativity;
8.   of the existence of subcultures and countercultures.

TOPICAL OUTLINE

I.   The Universality of Humans
    A. Same Species in Spite of Differences in Appearance
        1.   Differences Occur Because of Isolated Gene Pools
        2. People who Constantly Interact Develop Similar   Outlook

II. CULTURE
    A. Biological Predispositions to Culture
    B. The Birth of Culture
    C. Cultural Evolution and Sociobiology
    D. What Is Culture?
    E. The Symbolic Nature of Culture
        1. The Necessity of Sharing Symbols

III. THE MOST IMPORTANT SYSTEM OF SYMBOLS: LANGUAGE
    A. Does Language Create Reality?

IV. THE CONTENT OF CULTURE
    A. Material Culture
    B. Nonmaterial Culture
    C. Components of Nonmaterial Culture: Cognitive and Normative

V. THE NORMATIVE SYSTEM
    A. Values
    B. Norms
        1. Imperfect Agreement

A. CHAPTER OVERVIEW

Although groups of humans may appear different in looks, we are all members of the same species. Groups look different from one another because of where individuals happen to be born and because their ancestors shared a similar gene pool for many generations. Constant interaction with similar people produces not only outward appearance, but also a shared outlook on life, or a **culture.**.

Humans' **biological makeup** predisposes them to **develop culture**. For instance, among primates humans alone are completely **bipedal**. Human hands with the opposing thumbs are ideal for grasping, holding, and manipulating even the smallest and most delicate object. Humans' eyes face forward, enabling them to operate together in a stereoscopic manner which allows people to judge distances accurately and to see objects three-dimensionally and in color. Humans also have a brain of massive size in proportion to the body that is much more complex in structure and function than that of any other animal. This complex brain enables humans to remember, think abstractly, and symbolize, qualities that seem to be uniquely human. A speech center in the brain also enables humans to use their vocal cords for speaking and communicating with one another.

The above are **biological advantages**. But humans must also overcome a number of **disadvantages** in the quest for survival. First, humans are much weaker than many animals, lacking the latter's sharp teeth or claws. Then, the human infant is completely helpless and requires a long period of maturation.

Finally, humans lack instincts and inborn patterns of behavior; thus, they must learn how to behave in the most advantageous manner.

A. FILL IN THE BLANKS:

1. A predisposition toward the development of culture may be found in humans'_____ _____.
2. Human hands are especially adept at _____, _____, and _____.
3. Stereoscopic vision enables people to _____ _____ accurately and see objects_____ - _____and in color.
4. The human _____is much larger and more complex than that of other animals.
5. The most important functions of the human brain are the abilities to_____ _____, _____, and _____.
6. A speech center in the brain allows people to _____ with each other.
7. Among human biological disadvantages are _____, a long period of infancy, and lack of _____.

B. CHAPTER OVERVIEW

Culture is a frequently misunderstood term. In a general way, culture **is the way of life of a people**. More specifically, culture is a **product** of **social interaction**; it **includes** all the accumulated **knowledge**, ideas, **values**, goals, and **material objects** of a society; it is **learned** by each member of a society during **social-ization** (the process of becoming human); it **provides individuals** with ways of satisfying **biological and emotional** needs through patterns and systems of organized behavior. Each culture is **distinct** from every other culture, but all cultures share important **similarities**. Finally, cultures are always in a state of change.

Culture is possible because humans can communicate by means of **symbols**, rather than through **signals** as animals do. Signals are biologically determined and genetically transmitted, so they cannot be taught. Symbols are signs that can be taught; they are abstractions that stand for realities whose meanings are agreed upon by all members of a group. The most effective **system of symbols** is **language**, although **gestures, music, and art** are also symbol systems.

Language is the most significant product of culture and is at the same time the foundation on which culture is further developed and transmitted. Language allows people to create the dimensions of time and space, and, through writing, to expand knowledge and allow it to accumulate. Language and culture are so interrelated that if a culture does not value a certain trait, there is no word for it in that culture, and people are not aware that such a trait exists. Language, then, **shapes reality**. However, the potential for acquiring language is innate and universal in humans everywhere.

B. FILL IN THE BLANKS:

1. Culture is the product of _____ _____.
2. Culture includes all the _____, _____, _____, _____, and material objects of a society.
3. Culture is transmitted during the process of _____.
4. _____ is learning to become human.
5. Culture allows people to satisfy biological and emotional needs through creating _____ of _____.
6. Symbols make _____ possible.
7. Animals communicate through _____ which are biologically determined and _____ _____.
8. The most effective system of symbols is _____ although _____, _____ and art are also symbol systems.
9. Language is the most significant product of culture: it allows culture to be _____; knowledge to be accumulated; and the dimensions of space and time to be _____.
10. Language shapes _____ because if we cannot say it, it does not exist.

C. CHAPTER OVERVIEW

Culture may be divided into a **material** and a **nonmaterial** component. The material component consists of all the products conceived and manufactured by humans from the beginning of time to the present. **Nonmaterial culture** consists of abstractions that include **knowledge, beliefs, values, and rules for behavior**. The two components cannot exist apart from one another. Nonmaterial culture may be further divided into a symbolic component (language), a cognitive component (knowledge, beliefs, technology) and the normative component (values, norms--folkways, mores, laws--institutions, and sanctions). The **normative system** is the most significant because it **explains** why **societies work as they do**. It consists of difficult to define abstractions, called values, which are evaluations as to what is good, right, moral, beautiful, or ethical, and thus desirable. **Norms are rules** that tell people how to act, think, or feel on given occasions. Norms that specify expected behavior in everyday, **commonplace** situations are termed **folkways**, a term coined by William Graham Sumner. Norms that prescribe behavior in **important** matters are called **mores**. Mores define the rightness of wrongness of an act and their violation is considered a crime against society. **Taboos** are mores prohibiting certain acts considered extremely repellent such as murder, incest, cannibalism. **Laws** are

formal codes of behavior binding on every member of society. They specify what constitutes deviation and punishment for it. Norms are internalized by most people, becoming their "conscience," but laws are not--they are needed in a complex, heterogeneous society where norms are not fully accepted by all. The reason for the importance of the normative system is that in a group setting most members must conform most of the time in order to avoid chaos and anarchy. A society must exert a degree of **social control**, and it does it through the normative system which is more effective than force or coercion. Norms are enforced through **sanctions** which are divided into rewards (**positive** sanctions) or punishment (**negative** sanctions), and which can be **official** (positive: public recognition; negative: jailing) or **unofficial** (positive: a pat on the back; negative: being avoided or yelled at). Norms are also followed by most people because we have a strong need to belong to a group and do not like being outcasts. Norms, however, are not universally obeyed: some people never learn them, and others break them knowingly. In addition, some norms in society represent **ideal** behavior which most people, in reality do not follow. Cultural norms refer to ideal norms, whereas when speaking about how people really behave, we use **statistical** norms.

C. FILL IN THE BLANKS:

1. The two chief divisions of culture are into _____ and _____.

2. All objects conceived and manufactured by humans from the beginning of human existence to the present are part of _____ _____.

3. Abstractions such as knowledge, beliefs, values, and rules of behavior are part of _____ _____.

4. Nonmaterial culture has a symbolic, cognitive, and _____ component.

5. The normative system consists of _____, _____, _____, _____.

6. Evaluations as to what is good, moral, beautiful and ethical are called _____.

7. Rules that tell people how to think, act, or feel on specific occasions are _____.

8. Norms may be further subdivided into _____, _____, _____, and _____.

9. Laws are needed in complex societies because _____ are not fully accepted by all.

10. The normative system is important because in a group setting most individuals must _____ most of the time to avoid chaos.

11. Conformity to norms is achieved mainly by a system of positive and negative, official and unofficial _____.

12. People also conform to norms because they have a strong need to _____.

D. CHAPTER OVERVIEW

Since culture is a **patterned system of behavior**, for the sake of analysis its structure can be further broken down. The smallest element or unit of culture is a **trait**. A number of traits that accumulate around an activity is a **culture complex**. And a number of culture complexes clustering around a central human activity becomes an **institution**. Thus, a football helmet would be an element of material culture, team spirit and a belief in winning would be elements of nonmaterial culture, the game of football would be a culture complex, and sport would be an institution in American culture. Institutions are **formal systems of beliefs** and behavior composed of **interrelated norms and culture complexes** centering primarily on the five most **pressing human needs**: to provide food and shelter, to regulate sex and continue the species, to maintain peace and order, to transmit culture to each new generation, to explain the unknown and give purpose to human life. These needs have given rise to the so-called five **pivotal institutions**: the family, the economy, government, education, and religion. Institutions provide ready-made solutions as to how to satisfy these needs.

D. FILL IN THE BLANKS:

1. The smallest element or unit of culture is called a_____.
2. A number of traits accumulating around an activity is a_____
_____.
3. Several culture complexes clustering around a central human activity is an_
_____.
4. Institutions emerged to offer solutions to _____.
5. The need to regulate sex and continue the species gave rise to the institution of the _____.
6. The five most pressing needs resulted in the emergence of the_____ institutions.

E. CHAPTER OVERVIEW

In traveling, it is easy to observe that societies and their cultures differ among themselves. There is a tendency for people to use the viewpoint of **ethnocentrism** which is an attitude of passing sentence on other societies according to the standards of one's own. All societies exhibit a degree of ethnocentrism; but when it becomes exaggerated it leads to misunderstanding and conflict. To counteract ethnocentrism, social scientists originated the concept of **cultural relativity**. According to cultural relativity, each culture is analyzed on its own terms, in the context of its own societal setting, without applying any universal norms or moral absolutes. Cultural **variation** has been explained on the basis of race and geography, but neither explanation is totally satisfactory. However, while variation is common and sometimes striking, there is also a great deal of similarity among cultures, which proves our common humanity.

Similarities common to all cultures are called cultural **universals**. Not only do societies share cultural universals, but they adopt one another's cultural elements, thus leading to change. When two societies meet, a mutual transmission of cultural traits, complexes, and patterns of behavior usually occurs, a process called **diffusion**. Other processes causing change in societies and their cultures include **discoveries** (introducing formerly unknown elements), **inventions** (new patterns created from existing elements of culture), and **planning**. If changes occur too rapidly, people have no time to adjust and a situation called **cultural lag** occurs. This is an inconsistency in the cultural fabric of a society that can create problems. In general, human cultures have survival mechanisms that have worked rapidly and efficiently to adapt humans to environmental changes.

E. FILL IN THE BLANKS:

1. Passing judgment on other societies according to the standards of one's own society is called _____.
2. To counteract the negative effects of ethnocentrism, the concept of _____ _____was suggested by social scientists.
3. According to cultural relativity, no _____ _____ nor _____ _____ should be used to judge another culture.
4. Similarities shared by all cultures are called _____ _____.
5. Change in societies occurs through _____.
6. Additional processes of change include _____, _____, and

_____.
7. In a situation of cultural lag, people have no_____ to _____ to change.

F. CHAPTER OVERVIEW

Uniformities and variations occur among the various groups that make up each society. This is especially true in contemporary societies that are **heterogeneous** because members are immigrants, or occupationally special-ized. A group that has distinctive features that set it apart from the wider culture of the society, yet retains the principal features of the general culture, is called a **subculture**. The term does not imply any inferiority to the culture at large; it simply distinguishes a subdivision of it. Subcultures originate because of racial and ethnic backgrounds of people, because of religion, because of specific occupations, and even around certain institutions, such as the military or government. Some groups in a society adopt a value system and goals that are in direct opposition to those of the larger culture. Such groups are not simply subcultures. They are considered **countercultures**. The basic difference between subcultures and countercultures is their attitude toward society. Subcultures for the most part reinforce the cultural values of the larger society while giving loyalty to a smaller group within it; countercultures reinforce their members' rejection of the goals, values, and norms of the larger society.

F. FILL IN THE BLANKS:

1. Uniformities and variations do not appear among societies alone, but _____them as well.
2. Contemporary societies tend to be _____because members come from different backgrounds and are occupationally specialized.
3. A group with distinctive features but with the same values and goals as the wider society is called a_____.
4. Subcultures develop around _____, _____, _____,_____, and certain institutions.
5. The term subculture does not imply any _____.
6. A group that rejects the society's values, goals, and norms is called a

_____.

TERMS TO REMEMBER

counterculture: A group that possesses a value system and goals that are in direct opposition to those of the larger society.

cultural relativity: An attitude of judging each culture on its own terms and in the context of its own societal setting.

cultural universals: Similarities common to all cultures. (Example: the existence of pivotal institutions.)

culture: The way of life of people in a society. The totality of all that is learned and shared by the members of a society through
their interaction. The product of social interaction and a guide for further interaction. Culture includes material and nonmaterial aspects.

culture complex: A number of related traits that accumulate around a specific human activity.

culture trait: The smallest element or unit of culture. In material culture, it is any single object. In nonmaterial culture, it is any single idea, symbol, or belief.

ethnocentrism: The attitude that one's own culture is right and that cultural patterns different from it are wrong.

folkways: Norms that direct behavior in everyday situations; customary and habitual ways of acting.

institution: A number of culture complexes clustering around a central human activity.

laws: Formal codes of behavior. Laws are binding on the whole society; they outline behavior that deviates from the norm and prescriptions for punishing it.

mores: Norms that direct behavior considered either extremely harmful or extremely helpful to society. They define the rightness or wrongness of an act, its morality or immorality. Violation of mores is punished by society.

normative system: A system of rules regulating human behavior.

norms: Behavioral standards that dictate conduct in both informal and formal situations; a set of behavioral expectations.

sanctions: Rewards (positive) or punishments (negative) directed at individuals or groups by either legal and formal organizations (official) or the people with whom one interacts (unofficial) to encourage or discourage specific types of behavior.

signals: Biologically determined and genetically transmitted responses to outside stimuli.

social control: The process by which order is maintained within society through obedience to norms--folkways, mores, taboos, and laws.

subculture: A group that has distinctive features which set it apart from the culture of the larger society but that still retains the general values of mainstream society.

symbols: Genetically independent responses to stimuli. Symbols are learned and can be changed, modified, combined, and recombined in an infinite number of ways. Language, music, and art are common symbol systems.

taboos: Mores stated in negative terms. They center on acts considered extremely repellent to the social group.

HOW MUCH DO YOU RECALL? TEST YOUR KNOWLEDGE.

MULTIPLE CHOICE QUESTIONS

1. "The way of life of a people" is a partial definition of:
   - a. a social system
   - b. society
   - c. culture
   - d. tradition

2. Culture:
   - a. is the largest social system
   - b. includes abstract and concrete factors
   - c. is the same in each society
   - d. is found among animals as well as among humans

3. The principal difference between people and other animals is that:
   - a. animals are larger and stronger
   - b. people communicate with symbols while animals communicate with signals
   - c. biology dictates human behavior while instincts direct   animal behavior
   - d. people live in families while animals live in troops

4. Symbols are:
   - a. signs whose meanings are communally agreed upon
   - b. biologically determined signals to outside stimuli
   - c. musical instruments used to convey dramatic emotion
   - d. expressions of instincts in humans

5. The birds and the bees behave in specific ways because:
   - a. they have their own culture
   - b. they learned by observation
   - c. they are guided by instincts
   - d. they are responding to a natural law

6. The most important element in the development of culture is:
   - a. cooperation
   - b. group activities
   - c. a warning system
   - d. language

7. Language is a significant invention because:
   - a. it makes possible a wide range of communication

b. it has allowed people to create the dimensions of time and space
c. it has extended the range of knowledge of the individual
d. all of the above

8. The cognitive component of culture:
    a. includes knowledge, beliefs, and technology
    b. is made up of rules for behavior
    c. consists of values and morals
    d. is part of material culture

9. "They designate any standard or rule that states what human beings should or should not think, say, or do under given circumstances" is a definition of:
    a. values
    b. mores
    c. beliefs
    d. norms

10. The normative system includes all **but** the following:
    a. values
    b. technology
    c. institutions
    d. sanctions

11. Folkways may be defined as:
    a. those norms derived from tradition
    b. folk wisdom transmitted through the generations
    c. norms that specify expected behavior in everyday situations
    d. norms that specify expected behavior in special, unique   situations

12. Social control in society is exerted through:
    a. force
    b. the people's desire to belong
    c. sanctions
    d. all of the above

13. Traits, complexes, and institutions make up:
    a. social structure
    b. culture
    c. society
    d. statistical norms

14. Which is not a pivotal institution of society?
    a. the economy
    b. education

c. the family
d. a hospital

15. Which of the following groups may be considered a counterculture?
    a. a gang of delinquent youths
    b. the Branch Davidians
    c. the Manson family
    d. all of the above

16. When we refer to how people really behave, we:
    a. use statistical norms
    b. refer to the ideal norms
    c. speak of mores
    d. use folkways

17. Ethnocentrism refers to:
    a. an attitude with which members of one society judge another society according to their own standards
    b. the attitude that cultures be analyzed on their own terms
    c. the attitude that certain values and practices are common to all cultures
    d. all of the above

18. "Feng shui" refers to:
    a. culture shock
    b. superstitions peculiar to the Chinese
    c. cultural superiority
    d. commerce among the Chinese

19. Pivotal institutions:
    a. arise from fundamental human needs
    b. include government, the economy, education, the family, and religion
    c. differ in traits and culture complexes from society to society
    d. all of the above

ANSWERS TO FILL IN THE BLANKS:

A. 1. biological makeup
    2. grasping, holding, manipulating
    3. judge distances, three-dimensionally
    4. brain
    5. think abstractly, remember, symbolize
    6. communicate
    7. weakness, instincts

B.   1. social interaction
        2. knowledge, values, ideas, goals
        3. socialization
        4. socialization
        5. patterns or systems, behavior
        6. culture
        7. signals, genetically transmitted
        8. language, gestures, music
        9. transmitted, created
        10. reality

C.   1. material and nonmaterial
        2. material culture
        3. nonmaterial culture
        4. normative
        5. values, norms, institutions, sanctions
        6. values
        7. norms
        8. folkways, mores, taboos, and laws
        9. norms
        10. conform
        11. sanctions
        l2. belong

D.   1. trait
        2. culture complex
        3. institution
        4. pressing human needs
        5. family
        6. pivotal

E.   1. ethnocentrism
        2. cultural relativity
        3. universal norms, moral absolutes
        4. cultural universals
        5. diffusion
        6. invention, discovery, planning
        7. time to adjust

F.   1. within
        2. heterogeneous
        3. subculture
        4. race, religion, nationality, occupation

5. inferiority
6. counterculture

ANSWERS TO MULTIPLE CHOICE QUESTIONS:

1. c
2. b
3. b
4. a
5. c
6. d
7. d
8. a
9. d
10. b
11. c
12. d
13. b
14. d
15. d
16. a
17. a
18. b
19. a

CHAPTER 4

INTERACTION: FROM TWO TO MILLIONS

In this chapter, you will learn that

1. humans are group animals who achieve survival and acquire their human nature as a result of being members of one group or another;
2. within each group, individuals are assigned statuses and carry out roles, a condition that makes of each group a social system;
3. the existence of a social system gives life predictability, so that each social situation does not continually have to be resolved anew;
4. there is a multitude and variety of groups, but that primary groups are those most important to the individual;
5. the largest group to which people belong is society;
6. there has been a trend away from the small, traditional societies of the past (Gemeinshafts) to the large associational societies (Gesellschafts) of the present;
7. the interaction that occurs within all social groups is based on the processes of exchange, cooperation, competition, and conflict;
8. that the way to manage life in large, complex societies is through the establishment of formal organizations which depend on bureaucracy to function.

TOPICAL OUTLINE

I. THE SOCIAL SYSTEM: STRUCTURE AND ORGANIZATION
    A. Elements of Social Structure: Statuses and Roles
        1. Statuses: Ascribed and Achieved
        2. The Multiplicity of Statuses and Roles
            a. Roles: Real and Ideal
            b. Conflict, Strain, and Confusion in Roles

II. GROUPS
    A. Group Size
    B. Primary and Secondary Groups
    C. Additional Classification of Groups

III. SOCIETY
    A. Classification of Societies
        1. According to the Chief Mode of Subsistence
            a. The hunting and gathering society
            b. The pastoral, or herding society
            c. The horticultural society

A. CHAPTER OVERVIEW

Because human infants are born **helpless** and must depend on an adult for basic survival, the human way of life is above all a **group way of life**. Living in groups has forced people to create systems of behavior based on communication of individuals within a group. Communication between two or more persons by means of symbols (language) is the basis of interaction, and is called **symbolic interaction**.

Interaction, through repetition, acquires definite **patterns**, which eventually become a system. Thus, it can be said that human life takes place within a social system. A **social system** is a model used by social scientists to illustrate how social relationships work in a society. The social system of any group has a **structure** and an **organization** which consist of the network of organized relationships among the individuals who make up the social system. A social system is not structured and organized into a fixed set of rules; rather, the processes that take place in it are dynamic, and stable and predictable patterns of behavior are continually redefined to fit conditions.

One way in which the social system functions is that individuals in a group have specific statuses and fulfill definite roles. A **status** is a **position** in a social group that implies **ranking** or value rating according to the values prevalent in the group. **Examples** of statuses are: mother, teacher, son, students, etc. What the individual holding the status **does** is his/her role. Status and role, then, are the two sides of the same coin. They come into existence because a group (society is a group) needs to have certain tasks performed for survival, and it is more efficient to have specific individuals perform specific tasks.

Individuals are **born** with some statuses--they are males or females, for instance; we say that these statuses and the roles attached to them are **ascribed**. Other statuses are **acquired**: we get married and become husband and wife; and we say such statuses are **achieved**.

Each individual has a **multiplicity** of statuses and fulfills a number of roles. The status most important to the individual and the group is called his/her **master status**. The large number of roles that people are called upon to play create **confusion** and **conflict** for some individuals; thus, faulty role performance is not infrequent, leading to mental illness, maladjustment, and general frustration.

A. FILL IN THE BLANKS:

1. Life in groups forces people to create a system of behavior based on
_____.

2. Communication between two or more persons by means of language or gestures is called _____.

3. A social system is a model that illustrates how _____
_____work in society.

4. Repeated interaction gives rise to _____of behavior which then are the base of the _____ _____.

5. Any social system has _____and _____.

6. The members of a social system have _____and fulfill
_____.

7. A position in a social group implying ranking and value rating is a
_____.

8. There is no role without a _____because role is what the person holding the status _____.

9. Statuses with which individuals are born are called _____.

10. Acquired statuses are called _____.

11. Individuals hold a _____of _____and fill many
_____.

12. The most important status an individual holds is called the
_____ status.
13. The large number of roles creates_____ _____ and
_____.

B. CHAPTER OVERVIEW

In its sociological sense, the term **"group"** differs from an **aggregate**--which is a number of people who congregate in the same place at the same time--and **category**--which refers to a number of people who share the same characteristic. A group is composed of people among whom **symbolic interaction** takes place; there is recognition or **awareness** of group membership; there exists a degree of **consensus** about values, rules, and goals; and in which a **social structure** is evident, with members recognizing statuses, roles, obligations and privileges resulting from membership.

In most societies, there is an extraordinarily large number of groups. Therefore, classification is necessary. Some social scientists classify groups according to **size**: there are **dyads**, composed of two, and **triads** composed of three members. Small groups, such as families and friendship cliques, are the most important to the individual. Other classifications include those into **"in-group"**--people who are on our side, and **"out-group"**--all the others; **reference groups**, consisting of people whom we admire and whom we aspire to imitate; **voluntary** and **involuntary** membership groups--those we join for fun or profit, such as a runners' club, or those we are drafted into, such as the armed forces.

The most **important** classification, however, is into **primary** and **secondary** groups. A primary group is one that is relatively **small**, whose members are physically **close**, in which there is **intense interaction**, and which is fairly **stable** and of **long duration**. A **secondary** group tends to be **large**, and interaction within it is **short** and **businesslike**. Primary groups are very important to individuals: they represent their best support system. In modern societies, however, most interaction takes place in secondary groups.

B. FILL IN THE BLANKS:

1. An aggregate or a category of people is not the same as a _____of people.
2. To constitute a group, people must engage in _____
_____, be aware of _____ _____, and have a consensus on _____, _____, and _____.
3. One classification of groups is according to _____.

4. Groups that are most important to the individual are:_____, _____-
_____, _____.
5. Other classifications include: _____,_____,
_____, and _____.
6. The most important classification is into _____ and _____
groups.
7. A small group, in which there is intense interaction, which is fairly stable and
durable, is a _____group.
8. Short, businesslike interaction is typical of _____ groups.
9. _____groups are most common in modern industrial societies, but

C. Chapter Overview

Society is the **largest** group of people inhabiting a specific territory and **sharing**
a common **culture** and **social structure**. It consists of the **interrelated network**
of social relationships that exist in the largest social system. Modern societies
are generally nation-states, but in the past they were clans, or tribes, or large
families.

Societies may be **classified** according to their **mode of subsistence** or
according to their **social organization**. In the first kind of classification,
historically there have been the following kinds of societies: hunting and
gathering, pastoral, horticultural, agrarian, preindustrial, and industrial. **Industrial**
societies are characterized by **urbanization**, massive **mechanization** and
automation, complex **bureaucratization**, separation of institutional forms, and
substitution of **impersonal** ties for kinship ties.

A more frequent classification is the one according to basic **patterns of social**
organization. In this type of classification, societies are placed on the two extremes of an ideal continuum. At one extreme there is the **Gemeinschaft** society,
also called traditional or communal, with the following characteristics: small size,
little division of labor, the family as the focal unit of society, primary social
relationships, patterns of behavior dictated by custom and tradition, homogeneity,
with the society acting as an integrated social unit. At the other extreme there is
the **Gesellschaft** society, also called the modern industrial or associational, with
the opposite characteristics: large size, a complex system of division of labor, a
large number of social institutions and occupational, political, and social groups.
Relationships are of a **secondary** nature, patterns of behavior are regulated by
formal and informal laws, the society is heterogeneous and multigroup, with
diminished unity. There has been a visible **trend**, beginning with the late Middle
Ages, for societies to shift **from** the **communal** toward the **associational** kind.

C. FILL IN THE BLANKS:

1. The largest group inhabiting a specific territory whose members share a common culture and social structure is _____.
2. Society is the largest _____ _____.
3. Members of society are involved in an interrelated network of

_____ _____.
4. Clans, tribes, and large families have been replaced by

_____ _____ in modern times.
5. Societies can be classified either according to their_____ or their

_____ ___ _____.
6. Some of the societies classified according to their mode of subsistence
include: _____, _____ _____-

_____,_____,_____.
7. Industrial societies are characterized by: _____,

_____and _____.
8. A more common classification is into the basic patterns of

_____ _____.
9. Placed on an ideal continuum, the two opposite kinds of societies are
_____ and _____.
10. Some of the characteristics of communal societies are:

_____, _____ _____.
11. The characteristics of modern industrial societies   include:

_____, _____, _____.

D. CHAPTER OVERVIEW

Individuals in groups continually interact. **Interaction** is **symbolic** behavior, consisting of **words** or **gestures**. It is directed toward others and takes into consideration the reactions of others. Through repetition, interaction has acquired certain **patterns**. These patterns, called **social processes**, are said to be the chief elements of the social bond. The four **primary social processes** are **exchange, cooperation, competition, and conflict**. All other social processes are combinations of or derivations from the above.
Exchange is a transaction in which one of two individuals, groups, or societies does something for the other with the expectation of obtaining something in return of equal value. **Cooperation** involves two or more persons or groups working jointly in a common enterprise for a shared goal. **Competition** occurs when two or more individuals or groups try to take possession of the same scarce resource, tangible or intangible. **Conflict** is a hostile struggle between two or more individuals or groups for an object or value prized by each. These processes sometimes occur together, in the same interactive situation.

In a group setting, individuals must submit to some type of **order** or **control**. Society has been said to be the structure that imposes order on human experience. **Social control** is an outgrowth of social organization: it **results** when individuals **fulfill** the **roles** that go with their **statuses**. Thus, group life limits individual freedom in that if individuals do not fulfill their roles, tasks do not get done and chaos reigns. But freedom is of no use to the individual outside of a group.

D. FILL IN THE BLANKS:

1. Within groups, individuals are continually _____.
2. Interaction is of a _____ nature.
3. Symbols consist of _____ and _____.
4. Repeated patterns of interaction are called_____ _____.
5. The three primary social processes are _____, _____, and _____.
6. Individuals must submit to a degree of _____ in a group setting.
7. _____acts as the structure that imposes order on human experience.
8. Social control is the result of _____ _____.
9. Group life limits _____ _____.
10. Individuals must fulfill their _____ in order for social order to exist.

E. CHAPTER OVERVIEW

As societies become larger, more **complex**, and more heterogeneous, a **greater** extent of **organization** is necessary to channel, regulate, and direct those activities that in simple societies are directed by tradition and shared norms. One way of organizing activities efficiently is **through formal organizations**. Formal organizations are **groups** which exist for the **purpose** of achieving a **specific goal**. The **methods** by which formal organizations function--**bureaucracies**--are fixed so that they may be routinely repeated and performed by a number of different individuals. The **characteristics** of formal organizations are a **formal structure** in which systems and roles are fairly static and predetermined; **relative permanence**; a **hierarchical order** of authority; and a formal **program** in the activities and interrelationships of members, which are **systematic** and conform to abstract guidelines. Some formal organizations are joined by necessity; others, by **choice**. The latter are called **voluntary organizations**.

Large-scale formal organizations are administered according to the principles of bureaucracy. **Bureaucracy** is a **hierarchical system** for **coordinating** rationally the work of many individuals through division of labor and a chain of authority.

Max Weber, an early sociologist, determined that bureaucracy in its **pure** form--that is, the **ideal** form--should contain the following characteristics: specialization, a chain of command, a body of rules, impersonality, and selection based on merit and job tenure. In Weber's view, bureaucratic organization is one in which specific goals can be attained rapidly and efficiently and with a minimum amount of conflict.

In reality, however, bureaucracies **do not work** as well as they should. Some problems: they become resistant to change; rules become rigid; the top layers of the hierarchy obstruct changes that are perceived as threats; they tend to initiate policies instead of implementing them; they try to perpetuate themselves, extending size and influence; members may forge alliances with special interest groups and/or politicians; mistakes can be attributed to the next lower rung of the hierarchy; and a kind of **immortality** develops, since few bureaucracies are ever terminated, yet new ones continually come into existence. At the same time, bureaucracies have a **dynamic** quality that enable them to respond to changing conditions in society, and they are sometimes **instrumental** in promoting innovation and translating the ideas of scientists into manufacturing and distributing products. Finally, although the bureaucracy of large organizations encourages attitudes of impersonality and formality, **informal networks** of personal relationships develop within this framework, sometimes defying the purposes of the formal organization, but in the long run **benefiting** it.

E. FILL IN THE BLANKS:

1. While most activities in traditional societies are directed by tradition, in complex societies efficient organization is achieved through_____
_____.

2. Formal organizations are _____existing for the specific purpose of _____ _____.

3. The method of administration of formal organizations is called _____.

4. Formal organizations are characterized by _____ _____,_____ _____,_____ _____ _____, and a_____ _____.

5. Bureaucracy is a system for administering_____ ___ _____.

6. Bureaucracy is a _____system for coordinating _____the work of many individuals through division of_____ _____and a chain of _____.

7. The "pure" bureaucracy should consist of: _____,_____, a body of _____, _____, and selection based on_____ and_____ _____.

8. Some problems of bureaucracies include: a resistance to

_____, rigidity of _____, attempt at increasing _____and
_____.

9. Bureaucracies also contain elements of _____which promotes change and innovation in society and _____,which works to the organizations' ultimate benefit.

TERMS TO REMEMBER

achieved status: A position attained through individual effort or merit.

aggregate: A number of people who are in the same place at the same time, but who do not interact with one another.

ascribed status: An inherited position--one that is not attained through individual effort or merit.

bureaucracy: The hierarchical system of administration prevailing within a formal organization. The hierarchy depends on job specialization, a set of rules and standards to promote uniformity, and an attitude of impersonal impartiality.

category: (Referring to people) A number of people who have some characteristics in common but who do not interact with one another.

competition: A social process (form of interaction) that occurs when two or more individuals try to obtain possession of the same scarce object or intangible value using rules and limits.

conflict: A social process (interaction) consisting of a hostile struggle in which two or more persons engage for an object or value that each prizes, possibly to the point of destruction.

cooperation: A basic social process (interaction) involving two or more individuals or groups working jointly in a common enterprise for a shared goal.

dyad: The smallest type of group consisting of two members.

exchange: Exchange is the social process consisting of a transaction in which one of two individuals--or groups, or societies--does something for the other with the expectation of receiving something of equal value in return.

formal organizations: Large-scale associations of people in which most of the activities of complex societies are handled. They are highly organized groups displaying a formal structure, a body of officers, the expectation of permanence, and a hierarchical organization of authority (bureaucracy).

gemeinschaft: A small, homogeneous, communal, and traditional society. Relationships among members are personal, informal, and face-to-face, and behavior is dictated by tradition.

gesellschaft: A large, heterogeneous society, typified by the modern industrial state. Relationships among members tend to be impersonal, formal, contractual, functional, and specialized. Also called an associational society.

group: A number of people who engage in symbolic interaction; who are mutually aware of and influence one another; who recognize their membership in the group and are in turn recognized as members by the group; who are aware of the roles, duties, obligations, and privileges of membership; and who agree to a point about the behavioral guidelines, values, and goals they share.

in-group: Group to which the individual belongs and which confers on the individual a social identity.

out-group: Group to which others belong, excluding the individual defining group membership.

organization: A formal process that deliberately brings into existence a group of people to perform tasks directed at achieving a specific goal. It allows people who are unacquainted with each other to cooperate on complex projects effectively.

primary group: A relatively small group of people who live physically near one another and who interact intensely. Characteristics include stability, relatively long duration, informal and spontaneous interaction; and individual, personal, and total types of dealings.

reference group: A group providing individuals with standards against which to measure themselves.

role: The carrying out of a status. A way of behaving that befits a status and is transmittable as well as fairly predictable.

secondary group: A group that is in general larger and of shorter duration than a primary group. Interaction among members is formal, role-based, utilitarian, specialized, and temporary.

social organization: The network of patterned human behavior that is the product of interaction and that, at the same time, guides interaction.

social processes: Key patterns of interaction common to all human societies (cooperation, competition, and conflict).

social structure: The content of the social system, consisting of statuses, roles, groups, norms, and institutions.

social system: A conceptual model of social relationships in which each part is interdependent and interconnected to every other part.

society: The largest social group. An interrelated network of social relationships that exist within the boundaries of the largest social system.

status: A ranked position in a social group. Statuses are rated according to their importance in a social group.

symbolic interaction: Communication through speech, gestures, writing, or even music.

total institution an extreme type of coercive organization which isolates individuals from the rest of society, with the goal of changing their attitudes and behavior, and especially the sense of self, or personality, of the individual.

triad: A group consisting of three individuals. A more stable social unit than a dyad.

voluntary associations: Formal organizations that one joins by choice rather than out of necessity.

HOW MUCH DO YOU RECALL? TEST YOUR KNOWLEDGE

MULTIPLE CHOICE QUESTIONS

1. A number of people who find themselves together in the same place at the same time are termed a(n):
   a. social group
   b. category
   c. aggregate
   d. collectivity

2. Which item does not belong in a list of characteristics of a group?
   a. symbolic interaction
   b. reciprocal recognition of membership
   c. structure

d. affection

3. Which feature is needed for a collection of people to be considered a group?
   a. face-to-face communication
   b. personal friendship
   c. mutual adjustment of behavior
   d. awareness of common ancestry

4. The most elementary social unit is called a(n):
   a. couple
   b. dyad
   c. in-group
   d. individual

5. Which is **not** a characteristic of primary groups?
   a. relatively large size
   b. physical nearness of members
   c. intense interaction among members
   d. stability and duration

6. Within secondary groups, interaction tends to be:
   a. of short duration
   b. specialized
   c. formal
   d. all of the above

7. The form of interaction that occurs when two or more individuals try to possess a scarce object or value is:
   a. conflict
   b. coercion
   c. contest
   d. competition

8. Social systems include:
   a. dyads
   b. organizations
   c. life-style enclaves
   d. all of the above

9. Which statement is **correct?**
   a. Statuses and roles are one and same thing
   b. A status is a position, a role is carrying out of the obligations of the status

c. A status is what one does, a role is what one is

d. only some individuals have statuses, but all fulfill roles

10. Which of the following statements is **false**?

    a. Each person occupies only one status and plays only one role in society

    b. Each person occupies many statuses and is expected to play many roles

    c. All statuses are not equally important

    d. We are evaluated and ranked according to our master status

11. Bureaucracy:

    a. has always characterized all kinds of societies

    b. is the hallmark of modern industrial societies

    c. is a form of organization characterizing large, complex,   formal groups

    d. both b and c

12. Formal organizations that people join by choice are:

    a. institutions

    b. bureaucracies

    c. voluntary associations

    d. social groups

13 Horticultural and agrarian societies differ in that:

    a. agrarian societies involve the cultivation of grains

    b. horticultural societies create greater surpluses

    c. agrarian societies plow

    d. horticultural societies tend flocks and herds

14. Industrial societies are characterized by:

    a. urbanization, mechanization, and automation

    b. the substitution of primary relations for secondary ones

    c. the separation of institutional forms and the growth of complex bureaucracies

    d. all of the above

ANSWERS TO FILL IN THE BLANKS:

A.   1. communication

        2. symbolic interaction

        3. social relationships

        4. patterns, social system

5. structure and organization
6. statuses, roles
7. status
8. status, does
9. ascribed
10. achieved
11. multiplicity, roles
12. master
13. role confusion, conflict (stress)

B. 1. group
    2. symbolic interaction, group membership, values, rules, and goals.
    3. size
    4. dyads, triads, family and friendship groups
    5. in and out, reference, voluntary and involuntary
    6. primary and secondary
    7. primary
    8. secondary
    9. Secondary, primary

C. 1. society
    2. social system
    3. social relationships
    4. nation state
    5. social organization, mode of subsistence
    6. hunting and gathering, pastoral, horticultural, agrarian, modern industrial
    7. urbanization, mechanization, bureaucratization
    8. social organization
    9. Gemeinschaft, Gesellschaft
    10. small size, little division of labor, primary relationships
    (family focal unit, customs and traditions important, homogeneity, integrated social unit.)
    11. large size, complex division of labor, social institutions   (agencies, secondary relationships, heterogeneity.)

D. 1. interacting
    2. symbolic
    3. words, gestures
    4. social processes
    5. cooperation, competition, conflict
    6. order
    7. Society
    8. social organization

9. individual freedom
10. roles

E.   1. formal organizations
    2. groups, achieving a goal
    3. bureaucracy
    4. formal structure, relative permanence, hierarchy of roles, a formal program
    5. large-scale formal organizations
    6. hierarchical, rationally, labor, authority
    7. specialization, hierarchy, rules, impersonality, merit, job tenure
    8. change, rules, size and influence
    9. dynamism, informality
    10. unwilling, leadership

ANSWERS TO MULTIPLE CHOICE QUESTIONS

1. c
2. d
3. c
4. b
5. a
6. d
7. d
8. d
9. b
10. a
11. d
12. c
13. c
14. d
15. d

CHAPTER 5

BECOMING A PERSON : The Birth of Personality

In this chapter, you will learn

1. that human infants must learn how to become human beings;
2. that personality is based on a delicate interplay of heredity and environment;
3. that the acquisition of personality occurs through the process of socialization;
4. the various theories of socialization;
5. who the agents of socialization are;
6. that socialization occurs throughout a person's life;
7. that one has to become resocialized to each new role in life.

TOPICAL OUTLINE

I. PERSONALITY
    A. Personality: A Social Product on a Biological Basis
    B. Heredity and Environment

II. BECOMING HUMAN: SOCIALIZATION
    A. Goals and Functions of Socialization

III. THEORIES OF SOCIALIZATION
    A. The Looking-Glass Self: Cooley
    B. The Self in Society: Mead
    C. The Self and the Unconscious: Freud
    D. The Transitional Self: Erikson
    E. Developmental Theories: Piaget
    F. Moral Development: Kohlberg

IV. AGENTS OF SOCIALIZATION
    A. The Family
    B. The School
    C. The Peer Group
    D. The Media
    E. Occupational Groups
    F. Reverse Socialization.

V. RESOCIALIZATION

VI. SOCIALIZATION THROUGH THE LIFE CYCLE

A. Childhood
B. Adolescence
C. Adulthood
D. Old Age

VII. SOME CONCLUSIONS

A. CHAPTER OVERVIEW

Personality is a complex **system of behavior**, **thought, and emotions** that includes all of a person's attitudes, values, beliefs, habits, goals, and actions. It is **unique and dynamic**, in constant interaction with the external world throughout the individual's life. It is **circular**, affecting and being affected by the social structure. And it is **distinctive** because experiences exclusive to the individual are imposed upon a specific set of inherited traits and potentials.

Human infants cannot survive unless adults care for them until they reach a certain stage of maturity. Humans also have a strong **need** for social and **physical contact**, or love, remaining stunted or even dying when deprived of it. Finally, humans **lack** strong **instincts** and must learn how to act to satisfy their basic needs and drives. All these biological reasons **predispose** human infants to **accept** the culture of the society into which they are born. In the process of learning what the cultural expectations are, **each individual** newly born into a society also **acquires** a **personality**. This is done through the learning process of **socialization** in which the social and cultural heritage of the group is transmitted to the new individual.

A. FILL IN THE BLANKS:

1. Personality is a complex system of _____, _____, and
_____.

2. Personality includes all of a person's _____, _____,
_____, _____, etc.

3. Other characteristics of personality are the fact that it
is_____ and _____.

4. We say that personality is circular because it _____ and is
by_____ society.

5. Exclusive experiences and inherited traits ensure that personality is

_____.

6. The biological reasons that predispose humans to accept culture are: need
for_____ and _____, and for _____.

7. Each newly born individual acquires a personality through the process of

_____.

8. Socialization is the _____of a society's social and cultural heritage.

B. CHAPTER OVERVIEW

Not only is **socialization defined** as the process in which society's cultural heritage is **transmitted**, but it is also that **process** by which a **biological organism** becomes a **human being**. The central point in socialization is that new individuals learn from the people around them. Other people are necessary for an infant to grow up to be human. An **isolated** individual, who has never known humans, can **never** become **human**, develop a personality, or be aware of self.

The **specific aims** of socialization are: teaching the fundamentals of life; instilling aspirations, transmitting important skills, teaching to fill social roles. A person's **identity** also develops in the process of socialization which occurs, ordinarily, in the context of the family. Finally, socialization is not limited to infants and children, but continues throughout a person's lifetime, as people continue to adapt to new roles.

B. FILL IN THE BLANKS:

1. A supplementary definition of socialization is that it transforms a_____ _____into a _____ _____.
2. The central point of socialization is the need for_____ _____.
3. Among the specific aims of socialization are: teaching _____, transmitting _____, instilling_____ and preparing for _____ _____.
4. A person acquires his/her _____ in the process of socialization.
5. Socialization does ___ ____with childhood, but continues throughout a person's _____.

C. CHAPTER OVERVIEW

Personality **acquisition** has been explained with **theories** ranging from detailed expositions of how socialization works, to the well-known **psychodynamic** theories of Sigmund Freud, as well as the more contemporary explanations of modern psychology. Sociologist Charles Horton **Cooley** theorized that the self is developed in response to either positive or negative reactions of others to the individual; thus, the self is like a **looking glass**. George Herbert **Mead** saw the development of personality in terms of **symbolic interactionism** in which the infant first recognizes symbols, then acquires language, replaces actions with ideas, is able to think of self as an object, and finally, through significant others and game playing, internalizes the cultural values of the society, developing a conscience.

The **psychodynamic** theories are based on the view that biological drives are of central importance to human behavior. The term psychodynamic is interpreted as meaning that the behavior of an individual is motivated by mental and emotional factors present within him. The most significant of the psychodynamic theories is the one set forth by Sigmund Freud. It assumes the existence of **unconscious** processes that reveal themselves in **dreams** and in psychoanalysis. Freud insisted that an individual's **psychosexual development** occurs in stages, in the period from infancy to adolescence. The stages of psychosexual development are the oral, anal, phallic, latency, and genital. Each stage represents the individual's attempts to gratify the libido which is an instinctual drive toward pleasure that motivates human behavior. In the personality, the representative of the libido is the **id**, operating on a largely unconscious level; the **ego**, another part of the personality, functions on a conscious level forcing the id to satisfy its instinctual needs in a socially acceptable manner; and the **superego**, the third element of personality, exists to impose inhibition and morality on the id. The superego represents society and becomes an individual's conscience. Dysfunctions in the personality are caused by the disharmony among the id, the ego, and the superego which creates anxiety. In turn, anxiety leads to the development of **defense mechanisms**.

C. FILL IN THE BLANKS:

1. Personality acquisition has been explained by sociologists as occurring through _____ and by psychologists through the _____ _____ of Freud and others.

2. Comparing socialization to a looking glass, _____ _____ said that the self develops in response to the reactions of others to the individual.

3. George Herbert Mead saw personality development in terms of

_____ _____.

4. The psychodynamic theories of personality are based on the view that_____ _____are central to human behavior.

5. The most significant of the psychodynamic theories is the one proposed by

_____ _____.

6. The intriguing notion of _____ _____ that reveal themselves in _____ and _____is one of Freud's claims to fame.

7. Freud also maintained that psychosexual development proceeded in stages which are: _____, _____,_____,_____, and _____-
____.

D. CHAPTER OVERVIEW

Among the neo-Freudians, Erik Erikson (1968) contended that human personality development takes place in eight psychosocial stages which closely parallel

Freud's psychosexual stages. Erikson's stages, however, encompass the entire life of the individual and thus are more compatible with contemporary thought.

The **developmental** approach proposed by Jean **Piaget** holds that intellectual and moral development can only proceed in stages dependent on **physical maturation**. Developmentalists claim that people are active and capable of judging, interpreting, defining, and creating their own behavior provided they have reached a specific stage of maturation; they **stress free will and individual choice**.

Expanding on Piaget's ideas, the American Lawrence Kohlberg theorizes that children's **moral** development also proceeds in stages and develops from within the personality rather than being superimposed. Young children define right and wrong in terms of obedience and disobedience to authority: their morality is **pre-conventional**. Adolescents adopt a morality based on socially approved values, trusting in a higher authority: they are at a **conventional** level of moral development. And some, but not all, adults reach a **postconventional** level which acknowledges the existence of conflicting values and attempts to resolve rationally any value conflicts.

The **family** is crucial to socialization because it is able to influence the individual in the earliest stages of development; because it meets both **physical** and **emotional** needs of the individual; because it is a constant influence in the individual's life; because it is a **primary group**; and because it determines the individual's status, at least initially. Other agents of socialization are the **school**, the **peer** group, **occupational** or recreation groups, and the **mass media**.

D. FILL IN THE BLANKS

1. _____ _____ stages closely resemble those of Freud, but span the entire life of an individual.
2. Developmentalism holds that moral and intellectual development proceeds through _____ dependent on _____ _____.
3. The _____ is crucial in socialization.
4. Among the most important agents of socialization are: the _____, the _____, the _____, and the _____ _____.

E. CHAPTER OVERVIEW

Personality development continues **throughout life**. Since people's **statuses** continually change, they must constantly learn new **roles**. **Profound changes**, in which entirely new sets of norms and values must be learned and old ones forgotten, are called **resocialization**. Prisons and long-term hospitals require the most extreme instances of resocialization. But resocialization also occurs at all stages of the **life cycle**, in childhood, adolescence, adulthood, and old age, as well as during periods of **crisis** in individuals' lives, as in divorce, the death of a spouse, the loss of a job, or the onset of disability.

Stressing an attempt at **improving** personality in order to derive more satisfaction from life, rather than being concerned with how personality develops, are Carl **Rogers'** and Abraham **Maslow's self-actualization** theories. Rogers maintains that a person must have unconditional positive regard from others in order to realize his/her self. Maslow suggests a hierarchy of needs that must be fulfilled if a person is to develop normally and develop his/her potential. **Gestalt** theorists stress the totality of behavior and individual perceptions of reality as they affect personality.

E. FILL IN THE BLANKS:

1. Personality development is a(n)_____process because people continue to acquire new_____ and thus are forced to fulfill new ___-_____.
2. The process of _____occurs when new sets of norms and values must be learned and the old ones forgotten.
3. In addition, resocialization occurs at all stages of the _____ _____.
4. The most profound forms of resocialization occur in _____-_____.
5. Periods of crisis in a person's life also call for _____
6. Carl Rogers and Abraham Maslow are responsible for the so-called theories of _____ _____.
7. _____ theory stresses the _____of behavior as it affects the personality.

8. Carl Rogers and Abraham Maslow are responsible for_____ _____theories.
9. These theories stress the attempt to_____ personality in order to derive more satisfaction from life.

TERMS TO REMEMBER

developmental theories: A school of thought in modern psychology whose chief exponent was Jean Piaget. Developmentalists hold that personality development proceeds in stages dependent on physical maturation (sensory--motor, preoperational, and concrete- and formal-operational).

ego: (Freud) A part of the personality that functions on a conscious level. It attempts to force the id to satisfy its instinctual needs in socially acceptable ways.

generalized other: (Mead) The individual's perception or awareness of social norms; learning to take the role of all others with whom one interacts, or of society as a whole.

id: (Freud) The representative of the libido in the personality, existing on an unconscious level and making up the primitive, irrational part of the personality.

instincts: Genetically-transmitted, universal, complex patterns of behavior.

libido: (Freud) The instinctual drive toward pleasure that is the motivating energy behind human behavior.

looking-glass self: (Cooley) The process of personality formation in which an individual's self-image emerges as a result of perceiving the observed attitudes of others.

midlife crisis: What many people in middle adulthood experience when they reflect on their personal and occupational roles and find them wanting.

mind: (Mead) The abstract whole of a person's ideas.

personality: A complex and dynamic system that includes all of an individual's behavioral and emotional traits, attitudes, values, beliefs, habits, goals, and so on.

psychoanalytic theory: theory of personality developed by Sigmund Freud. It assumes the existence of unconscious as well as conscious processes within each individual.

psychosexual stages: (Freud) The manner in which individuals attempt to gratify the force of the libido at different periods of physical maturation. The phases are oral, anal, phallic (or Oedipal), latent, and genital.

resocialization: A process in which the individual's existing self-concept and identity are erased in favor of a new personality. Often, it is used as a requirement of a total institution.

self: (Mead) The individual's self-conception or self-awareness.

significant others: (Mead) Important people in an individual's life whose roles are initially imitated.

56

socialization: The learning process by which a biological organism learns to become a human being, acquires a personality with self and identity, and absorbs the culture of its society.

superego: (Freud) A final element of personality, existing largely on an unconscious level and functioning to impose inhibition and morality on the id.

symbolic interactionism: A school of thought founded by George Herbert Mead whose theories center around the interrelationship of mind, self, and society and include the belief that society and the individual give rise to each other through symbolic interaction.

total institution: An organization or a place of residence in which inmates live isolated from others and where their freedom is restricted in the attempt to resocialize them with new identities and behavior patterns.

HOW MUCH DO YOU RECALL? TEST YOUR KNOWLEDGE

MULTIPLE CHOICE QUESTIONS

1. The acquisition of personality occurs through:
   a. learning in school
   b. biology
   c. socialization
   d. maturation

2. Socialization is:
   a. a process that ends in adulthood
   b. a two-way process involving the individual and others in interaction
   c. the process of erasing a person's existing self-concept
   d. a form of brainwashing

3. The looking-glass self refers to:
   a. a theory of the emergence of the self
   b. the fact that we must look in the mirror to develop personality
   c. a theory developed by George Herbert Mead
   d. taking the role of others

4. Personality is circular and distinctive because:
   a. it dictates how we see our roles
   b. our roles affect personality

c. everyone has exclusive life experiences

d. all of the above

5. The family plays a crucial role in socialization because:
   a. it has the power to punish the child
   b. the child can only survive if its family takes care of it
   c. it influences the child at an early stage of development
   d. it has only a temporary influence in an individual's life

6. According to Freud, an individual's psychosexual developme occurs:
   a. in his or her infancy
   b. during adolescence
   c. in his or her maturity
   d. in five distinct stages from infancy to adolescence

7. The developmental approach to personality stresses that people:
   a. are basically passive
   b. can judge their own behavior provided they have reached a specific stage of physical maturation
   c. can be taught anything with the proper conditioning method
   d. never develop a full capacity for reasoning

8. Adults frequently undergo changes in personality as a result of:
   a. resocialization within total institutions
   b. occupational resocialization
   c. adversities in life experience
   d. all of the above

9. A self-indulgent playboy becomes a marine who is ready to die for his unit. We would call this change:
   a. reverse socialization
   b. resocialization
   c. secondary socialization
   d. remarkable socialization

10. Play is a critical element according to:
    a. Freud's psychoanalytic theory
    b. Mead's symbolic interactionist theory
    c. Merton's labeling theory
    d. Kohlberg's theory of moral development

11. Erikson maintains that identity crises:
    a. occur only during infancy through late adolescence
    b. can be successfully avoided

c. occur less frequently after adolescence
d. none of the above

12. Recent research by John Clausen:
    a. related success in high school to stable adulthood
    b. showed that some adults have very few crises
    c. concluded that most turning points in people's lives come before the middle years
    d. all of the above

13. Gestalt psychology:
    a. stresses human self-actualization
    b. focuses on the individual's perception of reality
    c. studies biological drives
    d. eliminates specific problems through conditioning

ANSWERS TO FILL IN THE BLANKS:

A. 1 behavior, thought, emotions
    2. attitudes, values, beliefs, habits, goals, and actions
    3. dynamic, unique
    4. affects and is affected by
    5. distinctive
    6. need for care, for love, and lack of instincts
    7. socialization
    8. transmission

B. 1. biological organism, human being
    2. other people
    3. fundamentals, skills, aims, roles
    4. identity
    5. family

C. 1 socialization, psychodynamic theories
    2. Charles Horton Cooley
    3. symbolic interaction
    4. biological drives
    5. Sigmund Freud
    6. unconscious processes, dream, psychoanalysis
    7. oral, anal, phallic, latency, genital
    8. learning, conditioning
    9. stages, physical maturation
    10. family, school, peer group, mass media

11. self-actualization

D.   1. ongoing, statuses, roles
      2. resocialization
      3. life cycle
      4. total institutions
      5. resocialization

ANSWERS TO MULTIPLE CHOICE QUESTIONS:

1. c
2. b
3. a
4. d
5. c
6. d
7. b
8. d
9. b
10.b
11.d
12.d
13.b

Chapter 6:

Deviance and Criminality:
The Need for Social Control

In this chapter, you will learn

1. that socialization is not perfect and cannot totally overcome the existence of deviance.
2. what is meant by the term deviance;
3. the functions and relative nature of deviance;
4. the various explanations of deviance furnished by the social sciences;
5. the nature, extent, and classification of crime;
6. the inadequacies of the criminal justice system.

Topical Outline

I. DEVIANCE
   - A. The Relative Nature of Deviance
   - B. Functions of Deviance

II. ATTEMPTS TO EXPLAIN DEVIANCE
   - A. Biological Explanations
     1. Body Structure
     2. Chromosome Configuration
   - B. Psychological Explanations
     1. Freudian: Insufficiently Developed Superego
     2. Overly Developed Superego
   - C. Personality Disorders
     1. Mental Disorders
     2. Psychosomatic Disorders
     3. Anxiety Disorders (Neuroses)
     4. Sociopathology
     5. Psychoses
        a. Schizophrenia
        b. Paranoia
        c. Manic Depression (Bipolar Disorder)
   - D. Treatment Of Mental Disorders
     1. Psychotherapy
     2. Behavior therapy
     3. Chemotherapy
     4. Hypnotherapy
     5. Electroconvulsive shock therapy

III. Deviance from A Sociological Perspective

A. Social Integration and Anomie
B. Cultural Transmission (|Differential Association)
C. Labeling Theory

IV. CRIME: DEVIANCE THAT HURTS
A. Classification of Crimes
1. Crimes Against Persons
a. Juvenile Delinquency
2. Crimes Against Property
3. Social Order Crimes or Crimes Against Morality
a. White-collar Crime
b. Organized Crime
4. Crime Statistics: How Much Crime, and Who commits It?
a. Gender
b. Race

V. THE CRIMINAL JUSTICE SYSTEM
A. Imprisonment
a. Recidivism
1. What Price Punishment?

A. CHAPTER OVERVIEW

Life in society requires a sufficient degree of **order** to allow peaceful coexistence. By performing the roles that go with their statuses and by obeying most of the **norms** of the society, individuals ensure that the **social system** works. Norms and roles are learned through socialization, but the latter is never perfect; nor are informal controls adequate in large societies to maintain social order.

Deviance refers to **behavior** that **conflicts** with **significant social norms** and expectations and is judged **negatively** by a large number of people. Deviance is **relative** to time and place, to who commits the deviant act, and even to who does the defining.

Deviance performs some **useful functions** in society: it strengthens nondeviants' faith in the value of conforming to social norms; it contributes to social stability; and it often heralds positive social change. On the other hand, **large-scale deviance** is damaging to the social order, and when it goes unpunished, it tends to **demoralize** those who conform to social norms.

A. FILL IN THE BLANKS

1. The fact that some people commit horrible acts may be attributed to a failure of _____.

2. Departure from norms that is _____ _____ is the definition of deviance.

3. Since it varies according to circumstances, time and place, age and mental health, we say that deviance is _____.

4. Deviants help define the bounds of permissible behavior; hence, deviance has a certain _____ in society.

5. Deviance is sometimes conducive to _____ _____.

6. The social order is damaged by _____ _____ _____, particularly if it goes unpunished.

B. CHAPTER OVERVIEW

Explanations as to why some people conform and others deviate from social norms have been offered by theorists from the perspectives of biology, psychology, and sociology.

Biological theories attribute deviance to **genetically inherited** flaws. **Psychological** theories attribute it to **mental or physical disorders**, while **Freudians** blame it on the imperfect development of the **superego**. Personality disorders include **brain disorders** or mental retardation which are physical (organic) in origin but may become emotional disturbances. In addition, disorders may be **psychosomatic** (unrelated to a physical cause) or may consist of **neuroses** such as phobias, amnesia, obsessive-compulsive reaction, and dissociative reaction. The most **severe forms** of mental illness are **psychoses: schizophrenia, paranoia, and bipolar disorder.**

B. FILL IN THE BLANKS

1. Psychologists assume that deviance is caused by _____ or _____ disorders.

2. Colitis, ulcers, hypertension, anorexia, and asthma belong to the category of _____ disorders.

3. Neuroses include_____ ,_____, obsessive-compulsive reaction, hypochondria, and dissociative reaction.

4. Psychoses include _____, _____, and_____ _____.

C. CHAPTER OVERVIEW

Sociological theories include the **anomie** theory (when there is a lack of balance in the social system and values are insecure, the individual responds with such deviance as **innovation, ritualism, retreatism, or rebellion**); the **differential association (cultural transmission)** theory (all behavior is learned in interaction with others in small, intimate primary groups); and **labeling theory** (which stresses the process by which individuals are labeled as deviant and their treatment as a result of that label). Labeling theory has a conflict perspective in that deviants are seen as victims as well as perpetrators.

C. FILL IN THE BLANKS:

1. Emile Durkheim introduced the concept of _____.
2. The _____theory of deviance includes such characteristics as conformity, _____, _____, _____, and rebellion.
3. A kind of _____ _____has been also termed the cultural transmission or differential association theory.
4. Primary and secondary deviance are elements of Howard Becker's _____theory of deviance.
5. Labeling theory considers deviants to be society's _____.
6. Labeling theory has a _____perspective.

D. CHAPTER OVERVIEW

None of the theories can be accepted uncritically; they all contribute to the explanation of deviance, but they do not explain its existence in **absolute** terms.

One form of deviance that is extremely damaging to individuals and society is crime. A **crime** is an action that has been defined by law as wrong because of its destructive nature. As such, it has been **prohibited** to members of society, and those who disregard the prohibition are punished. The chief **categories of crime** are **juvenile delinquency**, **social order** (victimless) crime, **white-collar** crime, **organized** crime, and **crime against person and property**--the most threatening and frightening category.

Statistics on crime are compiled annually by the FBI and published as the **Uniform Crime Reports**. The stress is on the **eight index** crimes consisting of **murder, rape, robbery, aggravated assault, arson, burglary, larceny, and auto theft.** These statistics reveal that those who commit crimes are largely **under 21**, **males**, **urban** residents, and blacks; but since only the unsuccessful criminals are arrested and most crimes go unsolved, undetected, or unreported, these statistics cannot be considered as totally valid.

D. FILL IN THE BLANKS
1. Theories that explain deviance cannot be accepted as _____.
2. One form of deviance that is very dangerous is_____
3. A definition of _____is that it is an act defined as wrong by law.
4. Disobedience to laws must be _____, otherwise there is risk of chaos.
5. The chief categories of crime are:_____ _____, _____ _____ crime, _____ _____, _____ _____ _____,crime against _____and _____.
6. Social order crimes are generally _____.

7. Statistics on crime are compiled by the _____ and published as the
   _____ _____ _____.
8. The focus is on the eight _____ _____.
9. The worst index crimes are _____, _____, and _____.
10. The characteristics of those who commit the most crimes are: _____,
    _____, _____.
11. Most crimes are _____.
12. The criminals who are arrested represent the _____.

TERMS TO REMEMBER

anomie Durkheim's term for a condition of normlessness. Merton used anomie to explain deviance, which he thought occurred when cultural goals cannot be achieved through legal institutional means.

bipolar disorder see manic depression

cultural transmission (or differential association) Theory of deviance (Sutherland, Miller) based on the proposition that all human behavior, including deviant behavior, is learned through symbolic interaction, especially in primary groups.

deviance Norm-violating behavior beyond the society's limits of tolerance

differential association See cultural transmission.

ectomorph In Sheldon's typology (biological theory of deviance), a thin and delicate body type whose personality tends to be introspective, sensitive, nervous, and artistic.

endomorph In Sheldon's typology, a round and soft body type whose personality is social, easygoing, and self-indulgent.

index crimes The eight crimes whose rates are reported annually by the FBI: murder, rape, robbery, aggravated assault, burglary, arson, larceny, and auto theft.

labeling A sociological theory of deviance that explains deviant behavior as a reaction to the group's expectations of someone who has once been decreed as deviant.

manic-depressive reaction A psychosis characterized by extreme swings in emotion from deep depression to a high degree of excitement.

mesomorph In Sheldon's typology, a muscular and agile body type with a restless, energetic, and insensitive personality

neurosis A mild personality disorder; an inefficient, partly disruptive way of dealing with personal problems, but seldom troublesome enough to require institutionalization. Neuroses include: amnesia, phobias, obsessive ideas or repetitive actions, and repression of thoughts or experiences

paranoia A psychosis characterized by the feeling of being persecuted or of being an important personage (delusions of grandeur).

psychosis A serious mental disorder in which there is loss of contact with reality. Requires institutionalization when individuals become incapable of functioning in society.

psychosomatic disorders Physical ailments developed as a result of emotional tension or anxiety.

psychotherapy A treatment for psychoses and mental disturbances that includes analysis, group therapy, family therapy, and others, centering around verbal exchanges.

reinforcement: The use of rewards and punishments to achieve a desired behavior.

schizophrenia A label for a psychosis that varies in severity from inability to relate to others to total withdrawal from reality.

sociopath A person suffering from a personality disturbance in which antisocial behavior does not elicit remorse.

HOW MUCH DO YOU RECALL? TEST YOUR KNOWLEDGE

MULTIPLE CHOICE QUESTIONS

1. Deviance is defined:
    a. in the same way everywhere
    b. in some cultures, as nonexistent
    c. in the context of time and place
    d. as another word for crime

2. According to Freud, deviance is caused by a(n):
    a. undeveloped Superego
    b. overdeveloped Superego
    c. unrestrained Id

(d.) all of the above

3.   An emotional disorder that allows one to work in society is called a(n):
      (a.) neurosis
      b. psychosis
      c. halitosis
      d. prognosis

4.   Schizophrenia is:
      a. another name for split personality
      b. a term meaning "to hallucinate"
      (c.) applied to a number of disturbances for lack of any other label
      d. a psychosomatic disorder

5.   Merton's use of the term "anomie" refers to deviance based on:
      (a.) lack of legitimate means to attain group goals
      b. mental retardation
      c. neurosis
      d. wild mood swings

6.   According to the cultural transmission theory, deviance:
      (a.) is learned in small, intimate groups
      b. is learned from books and magazines
      c. is learned from movies and TV
      d. transmitted in the culture

7.   Robert K. Merton views conformity as:
      a. an acceptance of cultural goals and rejection of the approved means of reaching them
      (b.) acceptance of both cultural goals and approved means
      c. habitual or compulsive pursuit of unacknowledged cultural goals
      d. rejection of both cultural goals and approved means of reaching them

8.   In the most correct sense, deviance refers to:
      a. any departure from social norms
      b. immoral behavior
      (c.) a departure from social norms that is perceived negatively by a majority of people
      d. any statistical rarity

9.   Who would not be considered a deviant from a sociological viewpoint?
      a. a "consigliere" in an organized crime family
      b. someone capable of solving complex mathematical problems at a young age and without much training

67

c. a supervisor in a public sector agency who uses departmental workers to remodel his home
d. a lawyer who defrauds his widowed client of the proceeds of her trust fund.

10. Which statement is true?
   a. All nonconforming behavior is deviant.
   b. A soldier who kills people during a war is a deviant nonetheless.
   c. A three-year old child who finds a gun and kills his brother is a murderer.
   d. None of the above is true.
   e. All of the above are true.

11. Which description fits the term *deviance* best?
   a. ambiguous
   b. scientific
   c. psychosomatic
   d. social

12. Deviance is more characteristic of:
   a. homogeneous societies
   b. heterogeneous societies
   c. subcultural groups
   d. uncivilized societies

13. An important function of deviance is:
   a. its contribution to social change
   b. its part in promoting societal stability
   c. to provide jobs for justice system employees
   d. all of the above
   e. only a and b

ANSWERS TO FILL IN THE BLANKS

A. 1. socialization
    2. negatively perceived
    3. relative
    4. function
    5. social change
    6. large-scale deviance

B. 1. mental, physical
    2. psychosomatic
    3. phobias, amnesia, dissociative
    4. schizophrenia, paranoia, manic depression

C. 1. Anomie
    2. anomie, innovation, ritualism, retreatism
    3. learning theory
    4. labeling
    5. victims
    6. conflict

D. 1. Absolute
    2. Crime
    3. crime
    4. punished
    5. juvenile delinquency, social order, white-collar, organized, person and property
    6. victimless
    7. FBI, Uniform Crime Reports
    8. Index crimes
    9. Murder, rape, robbery
    10. Young, urban, black
    11. Unreported
    12. failures

ANSWERS TO MULTIPLE CHOICE QUESTIONS

1. c
2. d
3. a
4. c
5. a
6. a
7. b
8. c
9. c
10. d
11. a
12. b
13. e

CHAPTER 7

THE GREAT DIVIDE: RANKING AND STRATIFICATION

In this chapter, you will learn that

1.	in spite of claims of equality, people are differentiated as to gender and age in all societies, and as to the amount of wealth, prestige, and power in societies that produce a surplus;
2.	the importance of such differentiation lies in the social meanings that are attached to it;
3.	ranking inherently results in inequality because it implies that some persons are or have more desirable attributes or things than others;
4.	where scarce goods are distributed unequally, a stratified system results;
5.	the theoretical explanations for inequality follow a conservative or liberal tradition;
6.	social scientists have developed several models of stratification systems;
7.	there is a variety of ways to determine social class;
8.	the consequences of social class and the factors involved in social mobility affect human lives;
9.	poverty seems to be an ineradicable kind of side effect of inequality.

TOPICAL OUTLINE

I.	Social Differentiation, Ranking, And Stratification
	A.	Stratification
			1.	Theoretical Views on Stratification
					a.	Structural-Functional Perspective
					b.	Conflict Perspective

II.	Dimensions Of Stratification: Class, Status, And Power
	A.	Class
			1.	Definitions of Class: Marx and Weber
	B.	Status
			1.	Status Inconsistency
			2.	Master Status
	C.	Power
			1.	Political power
			2.	Social power

III.	Systems Of Stratification
	A.	The Closed Society: Caste
	B.	The Estate System

A. CHAPTER OVERVIEW

Social differentiation refers to the fact that all societies differentiate among their members according to criteria that are given social meanings (Example: to be thin is good, to be fat is bad). To differentiate is to give **more** of the **rewards** of society to **some** than to **others**. Differentiation usually occurs on the basis of **social class**, of **ethnic or racial** origin, of **gender**, and of **age**. Differentiation is possible because individuals are **not equal**: they have different genetic traits, are born into different social classes, have different talents and degrees of intelligence, and have different socialization experiences. Although people are unequal and differentiated in all societies, in **complex** and affluent societies inequality and differentiation are **more evident**. The fact that inequality is recognized and differentiation accepted leads people to **rank** themselves from high to low. In effect, society is divided into layers, or **strata**: we say it is

71

stratified. The most common type of ranking, called **social stratification**, revolves around the amount of **wealth**, **prestige**, and **power** each individual has. Stratification is a consequence of the way resources are distributed in a society, and is **present** in **every society** that has produced a surplus.

A. FILL IN THE BLANKS:

1. All societies differentiate among their members according to _____ criteria with _____meanings.
2. The above means that the society decides what is desirable and what is not, and then _____among people.
3. Differentiation usually occurs on the basis of _____ _____,_____-__,_____ __ _____, and _____.
4. People are not born equal because they have different _____
_____, _____ ___ _____, _____ _____.
5. Inequality and differentiation are more evident in _____ and _____societies.
6. Inequality and differentiation lead people to_____ _____from high to low.
7. Social stratification is ranking according to the dimensions of _____, _____, and _____.

B. CHAPTER OVERVIEW

Social scientists are generally of the opinion that some social inequality is **unavoidable**. Theories of social inequality are derived from opposing philosophical positions: conservative and liberal. The **conservative** position, which held that inequality was part of the **law of nature** and a product of selfishness and greed, gave rise to the **functionalist** school of thought. Functionalists stress the **needs** of the **society** before those of the individual and maintain that in order for the tasks of the society to be carried out efficiently, a **system of rewards** must be instituted to lure the most talented and hardworking individuals. Functionalists also emphasize the need for **order, stability, and balance** in a society and claim that a system of stratification has a stabilizing influence. (Functionalism is also called the **equilibrium** theory.) Embracing a more **liberal** view of human beings, conflict theorists maintain that the natural condition of society is **constant change** which results from **conflicts and dissension** in the society. Such change, even though disruptive, is often **creative** and of long-range **benefit** to the society. Stratification systems, in the conflict view, are **mechanisms of coercion** because those in positions of power impose them on the rest of society as such systems work to their advantage. The best known conflict theorist, **Karl Marx**, thought that all of history was a record of **class struggles** because of the unequal distribution of rewards in societies. Moreover, societies are stratified because one group tries to protect its economic interest at the expense of the other groups. In particular, the **private ownership** of the means of **production** led to the division of society into the present social classes. Stratification is a technique of **oppression** of one social class by another, but it can also lead to the eventual development of a classless society once the **proletariat** (the working class) realizes that its own self-interest lies in rebellion against the **bourgeoisie** (the owners of the means of production). The two theories are not mutually exclusive: societies exhibit both stability and consensus, and conflict and dissension.

B. FILL IN THE BLANKS:

1. Social scientists believe that inequality is _____.
2. The conservative tradition held that inequality was part of the_____ of _____ and the result of human _____ and _____.
3. Functionalists are modern descendants of the _____ tradition.
4. Functionalists stress the needs of the _____ over those of the

_____.
5. Functionalists also maintain that a _____ of _____ is necessary in order to lure the best people to perform tasks needed for the good of the society.
6. Conflict theorists believe that _____ and _____ are the natural conditions of societies.
7. According to conflict theorists, conflict is beneficial because it leads to

_____ _____.
8. The best-known conflict theorist was _____ _____.
9. Marx thought that societies were stratified because _____ imposed the system on the others as it was in their best _____.
10. Marx thought that once the working class realized what was going on and rebelled, societies would become _____.

C. CHAPTER OVERVIEW

All stratification systems consist of **differentiation, ranking, institutionalization**, and the influence they have on individual personalities. In addition, they are all based on the **possession** of things that are scarce and therefore prized, things categorized as **class, status, and power**. People are assigned a rank in society according to these categories. **Social class** is an **aggregation** of people who stand in a **similar position** with respect to some form of **power, privilege, or prestige**. People belonging to any given social class display similarities in how they handle the experiences of life and in **life styles** sufficiently so that they become differentiated from others and come to constitute a **separate level**, (stratum). **Status** is the **ranked position** (high, middle, or low) of an individual **in relation** to other individuals within the social system. The rank is determined by how the role attached to the status is valued in the society. Status is very important to most people and affects almost all of our decisions.

In American society, social status is determined by **occupation, source of income, color, education, sex, age, religion, and ethnic origin**. The third, and possibly the most important, category of stratification is power. **Power** is the **ability** of one individual or group to **control** the actions of another individual or group, with or without the latter's consent. In short, power is the capacity to get other people to do what you want them to do. **Personal power** is the ability of individuals to direct their own lives; it is generally tied to wealth. **Social power** is the ability to make decisions affecting communities or the whole society. It can be held **legitimately** (as elected government officials) or illegitimately (as organized crime).

The concept of **life chances**, a term first used by Max Weber, helps to understand the importance of stratification to the individual. Life chances **refer** to the **opportunity** or **lack of it** that individuals have to fulfill their potential in society. Such opportunities are directly tied to the social class to which individuals belong: the higher the class, the more the opportunities, and vice versa.

C. FILL IN THE BLANKS:

1. Stratification systems are based on things that are_____ and therefore
_____.
2. People are ranked in societies according to the categories of
_____,_____, and_ _____.
3. Social class consists of a segment of people who stand in a similar position
with respect to _____,_____, and _____.
4. Status is the _____position of one individual in relation to other
individuals in a _____ _____.
5. Status, in American society, depends on _____, -
_____,_____,_____,_____, and _____.
6. Power is the ability of one individual or group to _____the actions of
another individual or group with or without the latter's _____.
7. People in full control of their own lives have _____power; those able to
affect communities or even the whole society have _____power.
8. Life chances refers to a person's ability or lack of ability to fulfill his/her
_____in society.
9. Life chances are directly related to the _____ _____.

D. CHAPTER OVERVIEW

The **class** system is a stratification system (others include **caste** and **estate** systems) that prevails in the so-called open societies. Theoretically, in an **open** society each member has equal access to material resources, power, and prestige. In reality, no existing society lives up to such an ideal, but the United States is one of the few that approximates it.

To determine one's social class, we use an index that measures socioeconomic status **(SES)**. Although most Americans tend to assign themselves to the middle class, around 2 to 3 percent are actually upper class (**upper upper and lower upper**). The lower uppers tend to be self-made professionals and entertainment figures and represent the achievement of the American dream. The middle class includes almost one-half of Americans and is also subdivided into the **upper middle, middle middle,** and **lower middle.** Although it is difficult to define, the middle class has become a **cultural symbol** in the society. The working class includes approximately one-third of the population and consists of people who work in **skilled, semiskilled, or unskilled blue-collar occupations** whose incomes generally fall below those of the middle classes. The working class is undergoing dramatic changes in the United States as a result of **globalization** and the shift of manufacturing to countries where labor is cheaper. But even in more stable times, this social class has always been subject to **layoffs and unemployment,** so that working people's financial situation has always been precarious. The Census Bureau listed 15.1 percent of Americans, representing approximately 37 million people, as living below the **poverty line in 1993**. Poverty in this society means a condition of having less income than the average person; we are not dealing with *absolute deprivation,* or not having enough income to provide the barest necessities for survival, but with *relative deprivation,* a condition in which people are deprived in comparison to others in their own society at a particular time and place. Poverty is chronic in families with a female householder in which no husband is present. The **working poor** are the percentage of Americans who work full time but earn less than the poverty level for a family of four. Additional social categories are made up of the **homeless,** the so-called **ghetto class** and the **new class,** categories that have originated in the past several decades because of the transition occurring in the economy.

Membership in a social class has consequences for the individual in all areas of life. Specifically, **life chances** vary greatly among the social classes, and there are striking differences in **child rearing, education, health, arrest and conviction rates, and values.**

D. FILL IN THE BLANKS

1. In an open society, every individual should have equal access to

   _____,_____,_____.
2. The class system is only one system of stratification; the others include

   _____, _____.
3. We can measure social class with the _____ _____.

4. The upper-upper and lower-upper social classes represent approximately ___to ___ percent of Americans.

5. Everyone's dream in the society is to become a member of the _____ _____ class because they represent the glamorous life.

6. The middle class encompasses almost ___ ___ of all Americans and is divided into the ____ _____, ____ _____, and ___ _____.

7. The working class is experiencing a great deal of discomfort as a result of _____, but it has always been subject to _____ and _____.

8. About ____ percent of Americans are described as living below the _____ _____, which means that they have less income than the _____ person.

9. Poor Americans are experiencing _____ deprivation rather than _____ deprivation.

10. Additional divisions into social categories include the working poor, the _____, the _____, the ____ class, and the _____.

11. The variation in life chances and lifestyles among the various social classes and categories include such areas as _____ _____, _____, health, arrest and conviction rates, and _____.

E. CHAPTER OVERVIEW

Social mobility in an open society is the individual's ability to **change social class membership** by moving up or down the ladder of the stratification system. In **vertical mobility**, the movement is up or down; in **horizontal mobility**, there is a change of status without a change in class. The American dream with its stories of individuals who have risen from poverty to extreme wealth is an example of the **myths** that have arisen about social mobility in the United States. Recent conclusions about social mobility are: that Americans frequently **move both up and down**, that there is more **downward** mobility than is at first apparent, but that more people move into the top levels of the class system than move out. Finally, **education** is a very important variable in upward mobility, and class origins are less important. Some upward mobility, in addition, has occurred not because of **individual effort**, but because of other factors: the increase in white-collar occupations, the low birthrate of upper-class people, allowing for an influx from lower classes for some jobs, the arrival of unskilled workers from rural areas and abroad forcing skilled workers into higher status jobs. Special talents are often the key to spectacular upward mobility, but at the **two extremes** of the stratification system mobility seems to be insignificant: at the top, there is an occasional downward slide, and at the bottom the lack of education and inappropriate socialization work against upward mobility.

E. FILL IN THE BLANKS:

1. Social mobility is an individual's ability to_____ _____   _____the stratification system.
2. In the United States, upward mobility is represented by the
_____ _____.
3. Research on mobility indicates that there is frequent _____up and down, that more people move _____ than it seems, but that more move _____than move
_____.
4. The most important variable in upward mobility is _____.
5. Upward mobility is sometimes spectacular as a result of _____
_____.
6. At the extremes of the stratification system mobility is _____.

TERMS TO REMEMBER

authority: Social power exercised with the consent of others. Parents, teachers, and the government represent different levels of authority.

closed or caste stratification system: A system in which class, status, and power are ascribed, mobility is highly restricted, and the social system is rigid.

conflict theory of stratification: A theory of stratification according to which the natural conditions of society are constant change and conflict resulting from class struggles. Inequality is the product of such conflict, as one group is victorious over others and asserts itself over the rest of society.

estate system of stratification: The prevailing system of feudal Europe consisting of three estates of functional importance to the society. The estates were hierarchically arranged and permitted a limited amount of social mobility.

functionalist theory of stratification: A theory in which social inequality is viewed as inevitable because society must use rewards to ensure that essential tasks are performed. The natural conditions of society are thought to be order and stability (equilibrium).

life chances: The opportunity of each individual to fulfill his or her potential as a human being. Life chances differ according to social class.

open or class society: A society in which the stratification system allows for social mobility and in which a person's status is achieved rather than being ascribed on the basis of birth. Open systems are characteristic of industrial societies.

power: A dimension of stratification consisting of the ability of one person or group to control the actions of others with or without the latter's consent.

social class: A dimension of stratification consisting of an   aggregate of persons in a society who stand in a similar position with regard to some form of power, privilege, or prestige.

social mobility: An individual's ability to change his or her social class member-ship by moving up (or down) the stratification system. Upward or downward mobility is vertical, whereas mobility that results in a change of status without a consequent change of class is horizontal.

social status: A dimension of stratification consisting of an individual's ranked position within the social system, the rank being determined mainly by the indivi-dual's occupational role.

social stratification (ranking): A process existing in all but the simplest societies whereby members rank one another and themselves hierarchically with respect to the amount of desirables (wealth, prestige, power) they possess.

stratification system: The overlapping manner in which members of society are ranked according to classes, status groups, and hierarchies of power. Analyzed on a continuum from closed to open.

structural mobility: Upward mobility caused by industrial and technological change that pushes skilled workers into higher status occupations.

HOW MUCH DO YOU RECALL? TEST YOUR KNOWLEDGE
MULTIPLE CHOICE QUESTIONS:

1.   Simple societies that do not produce a surplus may avoid:
      a. progress
      b. stratification
      c. conflict
      d. coercion

2.   Which forms of inequality are present in all human societies? a. sex
      b. age
      c. wealth
      d. all of the above

3.   People tend to rank themselves in terms of the possession of:
      a intelligence, beauty, strength
         wisdom, maturity, experience
         wealth, prestige, and power
         gender, age, hair color

78

4. According to functionalism:
   a. society must reward the most talented individuals for performing necessary tasks
   b. garbage collection is as important a task as medicine for a society
   c. a system of stratification is undemocratic
   d. the natural condition of society is conflict

5. Functionalist theorists:
   a. stress the needs of the individual
   b. stress the need for order, stability, and the importance of society over the individual
   c. hold that all positions in society are equally important
   d. maintain that there is no need for a system of rewards

6. Which is **not** a statement of Karl Marx regarding stratification?
   a. All of history is a record of class struggles
   b. Private ownership of the means of production leads to a classless society
   c. In every society, one group protects its economic interest against the others
   d. The proletariat must rebel against the ruling class

7. ". . . an aggregate of persons in a society who stand in a similar position with respect to some form of power, privilege, or prestige" is a definition of:
   a. social class
   b. status
   c. power
   d. life chances

8. What is the definition of "status inconsistency?"
   a. The condition of people who are ranked higher in one variable of status than in another.
   b. The order of importance given to status variables.
   c. The mechanism used by high status persons to protect themselves from competition.
   d. A situation in which individuals lack both money and a good reputation.

9. Power is the most important dimension of stratification:
   a. only in complex, industrial societies
   b. only in hunting and gathering societies
   c. in all types of social systems
   d. in all agricultural societies

79

10.	A person's position in the social class continuum affects his or her:
	a.	life chances
	b.	life styles
	c.	child-rearing styles
	d.	all of the above

11.	Power:
	a.	may be exercised legitimately or illegitimately
	b.	affects the distribution of society's goods and services
	c.	may affect individuals, communities, or societies
	d.	all of the above

12.	A class system:
	a.	works best in market economies
	b.	provides unlimited social mobility
	c.	is based on inherited titles and landed gentry
	d.	forbids inter-class marriage on religious grounds

13.	Which of the following is an example of the estate system?
	a.	classical India
	b.	the current plantation system of the American South
	c.	feudal Europe
	d.	today's United States

14.	America's affluent tend to be:
	a.	more liberal than the less advantaged on all issues
	b.	more liberal on many social issues
	c.	more liberal on many economic issues
	d.	no more liberal than the less advantaged on any issue

15.	By the "New Class," Barbara Ehrenreich means:
	a.	bureaucrats
	b.	career politicians
	c.	journalists, academics, writers, and media critics
	d.	all of the above

16.	While there is more upward mobility than downward mobility in the U.S.:
	a.	most Americans experience little mobility
	b.	real earnings have declined in some sectors of the economy
	c.	it has become harder to climb out of poverty
	d.	all of the above

ANSWERS TO FILL IN THE BLANKS:

A.
1. social
2. differentiates
3. social class, gender, race and ethnicity, age
4. genetic traits, levels of intelligence, social class
5. complex and affluent
6. rank themselves
7. wealth, prestige, power

B.
1. unavoidable
2. law of nature, selfishness and greed
3. liberal
4. society, individual
5. system of rewards
6. conflict and dissension
7. social change
8. Karl Marx
9. one class, interest
10. classless

C.
1. scarce, prized
2. class, status, power
3. power, privilege, prestige
4. ranked, social system
5. occupation, source of income, color, education, sex, age, religion, ethnic origin
6. control, consent
7. personal, social
8. potential
9. stratification system

D.
1. wealth, power, prestige
2. caste, estate
3. SES index
4. 2,3
5. lower upper
6. one-half, upper, middle, lower
7. globalization, layoffs, unemployment
8. 15, poverty line, average
9. relative, absolute
10. homeless, underclass, new, overclass
11. child rearing, education, values

E.	1. move up or down
	2. American dream
	3. movement, down, up, down
	4. education
	5. special talent
	6. insignificant

ANSWERS TO MULTIPLE CHOICE QUESTIONS:

1.b
2.d
3.c
4.a
5.b
6.b
7.a
8.a
9.c
10. d
11.d
12. a
13. c
14.b
15. c
16.d

CHAPTER 8: MINORITY STATUS

RACE AND ETHNICITY

In this chapter, you will learn

1. definitions of race, ethnicity, and minority;
2. how the majority has dealt with minorities in its midst;
3. the causes and effects of prejudice and discrimination;
4. some characteristics of the principal minorities in the United States;
5. that the United States is likely to become a different, multicultural society in the next century.

TOPICAL OUTLINE

I. Majority And Minorities
    A. Defining Terms
    B. Common Characteristics of Minorities
    C. Bases of Minority Status: Ethnicity, Religion, and Race
        1. Ethnicity
        2. Religion
        3. Race

II. The Making of Pluralist Society
    A. Ideologies Regarding the Treatment of Minorities
        1. Anglo-Conformity
        2. The Melting Pot
        3. Cultural Pluralism

III. Majority And Minorities: Processes Of Coexistence
    A. Segregation
    B. Accommodation
    C. Acculturation
    D. Assimilation
    E. Amalgamation

IV. In The Way: Obstacles to Pluralism
    A. Racism
    B. Prejudice
        1. Why Are We Prejudiced?
    C. Discrimination

VI. Racial Minorities

A. CHAPTER OVERVIEW

Social differentiation is not limited to the dimensions of stratification, gender, and age. Rather, it **includes** differentiation according to **race, ethnic background**, and **religion**. People belonging to groups that differ from the controlling group in society in race, ethnicity, and religion are called **minorities**. The term does not infer numerical inferiority; only the fact that as a category of people, minorities possess **imperfect access** to positions of equal **power, prestige, and privilege** in the society. Conversely, the dominant group, or majority, does possess access to high-status positions (although not all individuals reach them, of course); thus, its characteristics are considered desirable.

Because of wars or migrations, modern industrial societies tend to contain a number of minorities. **Racial minorities** differ **biologically**, so that differences are **visible**. **Ethnic** minorities differ **culturally** though they may be similar in appearance to the controlling group. **Religion** is often the cause for minority status.

Minorities have a **subordinate status** as a result of specific physical and cultural **traits** that the dominant group considers undesirable. They are aware of their differences and tend to stick together. They tend to marry within their group, at least for the first few generations, and minority status is inherited by descent.

A. FILL IN THE BLANKS:

1. Additional ways of differentiating people is according to _____, _____, and _____ if these differ from those of the dominant group.
2. The term "minority" refers to a _____ of people who possess unequal access to _____, _____, and _____.

3. Modern industrial societies tend to contain numbers of _____ because of _____ and _____.
4. Members of racial minorities are visible because their differences are
_____; ethnic minorities may look as the dominant group does, but their
differences are _____.
5. Among the characteristics of minorities are: awareness of_____ position,
_____together, marriage _____ ___ _____, status inherited by
_____.

B. CHAPTER OVERVIEW

At different times in our history, different ideologies expressed the feelings the
majority had toward the ultimate fate of minorities in the society. The ideology
with the greatest following originated from an attempt to superimpose white
Anglo-Saxon Protestant (WASP) standards and values on all minorities. This
ideology was termed **Anglo-conformity** and resulted in federal, state, and local
efforts to **Americanize** immigrants by having them learn English, abandon their
customs, become naturalized citizens, and finally by establishing immigration
quotas that discriminated against immigrants from eastern and southern
European countries.

The **melting pot** ideology developed during the l9th century when Americans
began to believe that many immigrants could make important contributions to the
United States. According to this ideology, it would be possible to **fuse** all the
various stocks, both biologically and culturally, to obtain a "New American." The
ideology proved unrealistic when it was discovered that **intermarriage** was
occurring according to **religious** patterns--with a Protestant, Catholic, and
Jewish pool being created.

Cultural pluralism is the ideology most **widely accepted** today. It stresses the
desirability of each ethnic group **retaining** its cultural **distinctions** while giving its
political and nationalistic loyalty to the United States. The ideal behind this
ideology has not been completely attained, but it remains our goal.

B. FILL IN THE BLANKS

1. A number of different ideologies have been popular in the United States
regarding the role of _____in the society.
2. The one that had the greatest following originally was the one termed

_____.

3. Anglo-conformity was based on attempting to have minorities become

_____.

4. A more idealistic ideology, popular in the l9th century, was called the _____

_____.

5. According to the ideology popular in the I9th-century, it was possible to create a _____ _____.

6. To create a new American, it was necessary to_____ both_____and _____the old stocks.

7. It was found that although the different immigrant groups did intermarry, they did so according to _____.

8. The ideology that allows for cultural distinctiveness in a national context is called _____ _____.

9. Minorities have coped with the majority in a variety of ways: through _____,_____, _____, _____, or migration.

C. CHAPTER OVERVIEW

Ideally, if all differences between minorities and the majority were to be eliminated, we would have an **amalgamated** society. In reality, minorities have reacted in a variety of ways to their status. Some have wanted to **retain** their previous cultural heritage while giving political loyalty to their new home and **coexisting** in harmony with the majority and other groups in the society; these minorities are **pluralistic**. Some have preferred to **absorb** the culture of the dominant group until they blended with it; these minorities are **assimilationist**. Some have given up their original language and traditions in favor of new ones; they have become **acculturated**.

The **majority** tries to maintain its high status by **establishing** and **enforcing** the **value system** and the **behavioral norms** for the society and considers deviant those norms and values which differ from its own. It also **obstructs assimilation** by institutionalizing its prejudices. Sometimes assimilation is forced; but generally **pluralism** is said to be the **goal**. There have been many instances, however, in which majority groups have expelled their minorities, or one minority, and resort to genocide (killing off an entire people) is unfortunately also familiar.

C. FILL IN THE BLANKS

1. Ideally, if a perfect blending would take place between majority and minorities, we would have an _____society.

2. In trying to maintain its majority status, the majority establishes and enforces its _____system and the_____ norms.

3. The majority also _____its prejudices.

4. The ultimate method of dealing with minorities is through _____.

D. CHAPTER OVERVIEW

The term **race** is subject to much **misinterpretation** (see Chapter 2). Scientists use the concept of race to describe **biological differences** occurring in the human species. People who share certain visible physical characteristics have been categorized into races. Unfortunately, in time customs and mental or moral characteristics associated with members of specific races were thought to be a function of race rather than culture and thus capable of being transmitted through heredity. Thus the term race has become a **subjective, socially constructed** perception of reality, and not an objective term referring to the distinction between biologically different groupings of people. **Racism** is the **ideology** behind this mistaken use of the term, being the **incorrect belief** that both **physical traits** and general behavior are **inherited**. The implication is also that behavior is inferior or undesirable. **Racist thinking** is based on **stereotyping**, or extending common, uniform characteristics to an entire group, without allowing for individual differences, and as an ideology differs from ethnocentrism (see Chapter 3) which is simply a belief in the superiority of one's own group.

Racism as an ideology has **declined** in the United States, but hostile feelings against racial groups remain. Because of the unpleasant connotations of race, a new term, **ethnicity** has become more popular. Ethnicity **refers** to a group's **distinctiveness** based on **social and cultural** factors rather than on biological ones. Heterogeneous societies are made up of a number of ethnic subcultures.

Racial and ethnic groups are often hostile to one another. The most common evidence of conflict is the presence of **prejudice and discrimination**. Prejudice is making up one's mind about someone before examining all the evidence and then refusing to change one's mind even if the facts do not support it. Prejudice is learned; it is thought to be encouraged by **insecurity, social isolation, frustration**, and the need to rationalize personal failure; it does not necessarily originate through contact; and it persists because it is emotionally satisfying. Prejudice may also be a psychological mechanism called **scapegoating**, which is a tendency of frustrated individuals to respond with aggression against a handy target; or **projection**, which is seeing traits in other groups that one secretly admires and wants to imitate but which are openly hated or feared.

While **prejudice** is an attitude or **feeling**, **discrimination** is **actions** taken as a result of prejudice. It is possible to have prejudice without deiscimination, and discrimination without prejudice, but as a rule the two **reinforce** each other. **Attitudinal** discrimination refers to a situation in which the rewards of society are **withheld** from target group members in spite of their qualifications. **Institutional** discrimination refers to the system of inequalities built into the society apart from the prejudices of individual members.

D. FILL IN THE BLANKS:

1. In its scientific sense, race is a term used to describe _____ variations in the human species.
2. People began to think that customs and behavior were capable of being _____ through heredity.
3. Racist thinking is based on _____.
4. Stereotyping is attributing a common trait to an _____ group, without allowing for _____ differences.
5. Ethnicity refers to a group's _____ _____.
6. Conflict between ethnic and racial groups is evidenced by the presence of _____ and _____.
7. Prejudice is making up one's mind without _____ and refusing to change it in spite of evidence.
8. Discrimination is _____ on the basis of prejudice.
9. Prejudice is _____; it is encouraged by _____ and _____ _____ and it persists because it is _____ _____.
10. Discrimination may be _____, and _____.

E. CHAPTER OVERVIEW

Native Americans, the original natives of this country, have been decimated by wars waged by the settlers on them, and by the diseases brought by the Europeans. Economically, they are the **worst off of minorities**, having a large unemployment rate and one of the lowest average family income rates. Most live on reservations, chiefly in the Southwest, though enclaves exist in some urban centers and in rural areas throughout the country. Native Americans are intensely **tribal** and have been the least receptive to European culture. Some American Indian groups have learned successfully some capitalist business procedures, and are prospering.

Asian Americans consist of Chinese and Japanese, and of late, of refugees from the Vietnam conflagration. Chinese immigration began in the middle of the 19th century, mainly to California, where many came to find gold and ended by working to build the railroads. They were heavily discriminated against and their immigration was restricted; in spite of this, as a group they have **achieved** great **upward mobility**, through education and habits of hard work and thrift. The Japanese began arriving toward the beginning of the 20th century, also mainly to the West Coast, and experienced the same sort of discrimination, as they were described by prejudiced Americans to be part of the "yellow peril." They, too, however, held **values** that assisted their upward mobility: they were hardworking, frugal, and valued education for their children.

The present-day influx of Asians was caused by the problems created by Vietnam. **Asians** are the **fastest-growing** ethnic group and hold the highest median family income, in spite of lack of skills and education. In some localities, competition with natives has created problems so that the government has begun to restrict immigration on the part of persons wanting to come not because of political oppression, but simply in the search for a better life.

African Americans make up approximately l2 percent of the population of the United States, the **largest minority** group if one does not count women. Their immigration was involuntary, one reason for their status as a special minority group. Because their ties with Africa were totally destroyed, blacks had to **create a new culture** based on the experience of slavery in the midst of the dominant culture. It is generally agreed that slavery was responsible for the negative self-image of most blacks and for the consequent problems it has brought to the black family and the social structure of the group. The civil rights movement has done much to remedy that image, and legislation, such as the Affirmative Action Act, has attempted to remedy the slights done blacks by the denial of many opportunities. However, while many blacks have indeed risen in the stratification system, mostly as a result of increased amounts of education, a so-called underclass consisting of unskilled immigrants from rural areas remains stubbornly on the bottom.

The **Spanish-speaking minorities** may be divided into Mexican-Americans, concentrated in Arizona, California and other western states, Puerto Ricans, concentrated in the cities of the eastern seaboard, and Cubans, concentrated in Florida, especially Miami. They do **not** constitute a **unified community**, nor do they have a common culture; but they do share a language and the Catholic religion. Mexican-Americans have a low socio-economic status, remaining in the ranks of unskilled and semi-skilled labor, chiefly because they remain **committed to Mexican culture**, retaining the language, and often returning to live after a few years of working in the United States. The Puerto Ricans have a similar problem: coming from an agricultural background, they can only offer **unskilled labor**, and most return to their native land after a few years. Both groups are becoming politically more committed to the United States, and their interests are consequently being better represented. The Cubans, who came following the revolution that brought Fidel Castro to power, are generally thriving because of their **middle-class professions** that fit in easily into a capitalistic system.

White ethnics are the descendants of the Poles, Irish, Italians, Greeks, and other Slavs who did not resemble the immigrants from Great Britain and Germany, and thus were subject to greater amounts of **discrimination**. Some of these descendants have managed to rise socially, mainly through educational achievements that propelled them into the **professional** sphere. Others, however, remained in the ranks of the working class, living in urban enclaves in which they have retained a close-knit community. They tend to be resentful of the help they perceive the government as having given to the other minorities while they subsisted on their low-income jobs.

D. FILL IN THE BLANKS

1. The largest minority group consists of _____ who have special problems because of having come here _____.
2. The negative self-image of blacks, as well as other problems, are attributed to the experience of _____ and the destruction of_____ _____to their native land.
3. The most problematic segments of the black minority is the so-called _____.
4. The Spanish-speaking minorities are not a _____but they share a common _____and _____.
5. The low socioeconomic status of both Mexican Americans and Puerto Ricans is partly due to their lack of _____ _____, and partly because they lack _____to American culture.
6. American Indians, the original _____ _____, are intensely _____ and least _____to European culture.
7. Chinese immigrants arrived in the _____century in search of _____, and found employment building _____.
8. Although considered part of the "_____" the Japanese achieved upward mobility because of such values as _____ _____, _____-and _____for their children.
9. The fastest-growing ethnic group in the United States are _____ who are achieving great _____ _____.
10. White ethnics are resentful of the help the government gives_____ _____groups.

E. CHAPTER OVERVIEW

Among the **religious** minorities, Catholics and Jews were subject to prejudice and discrimination at the turn of the century and into the first several decades of this century. These feelings of hostility may have been directed toward their ethnic origin--eastern and southern European--as much as toward their religions. In any event, both groups have done **well** socioeconomically, being represented among the **highest earners** and in the ranks of professionals.

The **dilemma** facing the United States is **how** to achieve **pluralism** without **conflict**, how to live up to the motto "E pluribus unum"--out of many, one--that we display but have failed to live up to.

E. FILL IN THE BLANKS:

1. The "American dilemma" remains how to make a nation of many into _____ entity.
2. Catholics and Jews were discriminated against mainly during the _____ years of the century.
3. Their discrimination was due more to _____ than religious factors.
4. Both groups, however, have done well in _____ terms.
5. They are among the _____ earners in _____ professional ranks.

TERMS TO REMEMBER

accommodation: A situation in which a minority is conscious of the norms and values of the majority, accepts and adapts to them, but chooses to retain its own, thus failing to participate in the host culture.

acculturation: The process of adopting the culture, including the language and customs, of the host country.

amalgamation: The result of intermarriage between distinct racial, ethnic, and cultural groups, resulting in the erasure of differences between majority and minority groups.

anglo-conformity: The attitude, once held by the majority group, that the institutions, language, and cultural patterns of England should be maintained.

assimilation: A process in which a minority group is absorbed into, or becomes part of, the dominant group in a society.

attitudinal discrimination: Negative behavior against a particular group--or individual members of that group--prompted by personal prejudice.

cultural pluralism: An ideal condition in which the cultural distinctiveness of each ethnic, racial, and religious minority group would be maintained, while individual members would still owe allegiance to the society in general.

discrimination: Actions taken as a result of prejudicial feelings.

ethnic minority: A group that differs culturally from the dominant group.

ethnicity: A group's distinctive social, rather than biological, traits.

ethnocentrism: Belief in the superiority of one's own group.

institutional discrimination: Negative behavior toward minority groups prompted by the knowledge that such prejudice exists on a societal level; that it is, in effect, a norm of the society. Includes structural form--found in structures such as government and the economy--and cultural form--in which the majority defines its own values, norms, attitudes, and interpretations of reality as the standards for the entire society.

melting pot theory: The belief that it is possible and desirable to fuse culturally and biologically all the various racial and ethnic groups in society.

minority group: Any group in society that is kept from attaining the rewards of society on the basis of culture, race, religion, sex or age. A category of people who possess imperfect access to positions of equal power and to the corollary dimensions of prestige and privilege in the society.

prejudice: Prejudgment of an individual or group based on stereotypes and hearsay rather than on fact or evidence, and the inability or unwillingness to change that judgment even when confronted with evidence to the contrary.

race: An arbitrary manner of subdividing the species Homo Sapiens based on differences in the frequency with which some genes occur among populations.

racial minority: A group within a society that differs biologically from the dominant group in such features as skin color, hair texture, eye slant, and head shape and dimensions.

racism: The belief that racial groups display not only physical, but also behavioral differences, and that both are inherited and inferior or undesirable.

segregation: An attempt to isolate a minority from the majority.

HOW MUCH DO YOU RECALL? TEST YOUR KNOWLEDGE
MULTIPLE CHOICE QUESTIONS

1. Membership in specific racial, ethnic, and religious groupings is:
    a. characteristic only of industrial societies
    b. a variable of the stratification system
    c. a biological rather than a social product
    d. the cross every individual must bear

2. The term "minority" may be defined as:
    a. a small group of people living within a large nation

b. a group of people who possess the same access to prestige, privilege, and power but who differ in looks

c. any group in society that is socially dominated by another group through discrimination because of race, culture, religion, sex, or age

d. any small group in society which is disliked and abused

3. The difference between racial minorities and ethnic minorities is:
   a. in the size of each group
   b. ethnic minorities do not suffer from discrimination, but only from prejudice
   c. racial minorities are differentiated by physical appearance from the dominant group, ethnic minorities differ culturally from the dominant group
   d. racial minorities are smaller in number than ethnic minorities

4. Minorities have reacted to domination by developing goals that may be called:
   a. pluralistic
   b. assimilationist
   c. secessionist
   d. all of the above

5. Conflicts between the dominant group and minorities develop because:
   a. minorities are perceived as different
   b. minorities perceive themselves as different
   c. the dominant group has coercive power
   d. all of the above

6. Dominant groups tend to use all **but** one of the following methods in dealing with minorities:
   a. forced assimilation
   b. cultural relativity
   c. population transfers
   d. economic exploitation

7. Scientists agree that:
   a. there are three races
   b. there are fifty two races
   c. there are no races
   d. all of humankind is descended from the same common stock

8. Members of an ethnic group:
   a. share behavioral traits
   b. share social and cultural traits
   c. share physical traits
   d. are heterogeneous

9. The term "prejudice" implies:
    a. that one makes a judgment before having all the facts
    b. that one refuses to change one's mind even when confronted by facts
    c. that one takes action against members of minorities
    d. only a and b

10. Which is **not** a reason for the low economic and social status of Mexican Americans?
    a. They are concentrated in agricultural and low-skill jobs.
    b. The nearness of Mexico leads to a retention of Spanish as the principal language.
    c. Parents tend to be ambitious and upwardly mobile which leads to rebelliousness in their children.
    d. The norms of their subculture do not encourage upward mobility.

11. The United States became a "triple melting pot" in that:
    a. racial, ethnic, and religious groups merged
    b. three racial groups emerged
    c. marriage among ethnic groups followed along the lines of the three main religions
    d. all of the above

12. The problems of Native Americans have been complicated by:
    a. tribalism
    b. lack of a common language
    c. the conditions on reservations
    d. all of the above

13. In Andrew Hacker's view:
    a. blacks have been given more than an equal opportunity
    b. being black remains the greatest stigma in this country
    c. blacks receive a disproportionate percentage of total personal income
    d. none of the above

14. William J. Wilson attributes the worsening conditions of the underclass to:
    a. a psychology of victimhood
    b. abandonment of the inner city by upwardly mobile blacks
    c. race-identifying protest leaders
    d. affirmative action and lowered educational standards

15. Latinos:
    a. possess a homogeneous common culture

94

b. constitute a unified socio-political community
c. are bound together by a common language and religion
d. overwhelmingly oppose bilingual education

16. In the Puerto Rican community, "va y ven" means:
    a. the movement to the suburbs
    b. commuting back and forth to work
    c. returning to Puerto Rico after living in the U.S.
    d. none of the above

ANSWERS TO FILL IN THE BLANKS:

A. 1. social
    2. differentiates
    3. social class, gender, race and ethnicity, age
    4. genetic traits, levels of intelligence, social class
    5. complex and affluent
    6. rank themselves
    7. wealth, prestige, power

B. 1. unavoidable
    2. law of nature, selfishness and greed
    3. liberal
    4. society, individual
    5. system of rewards
    6. conflict and dissension
    7. social change
    8. Karl Marx
    9. one class, interest
    10. classless

C. 1. scarce, prized
    2. class, status, power
    3. power, privilege, prestige
    4. ranked, social system
    5. occupation, source of income, color, education, sex, age, religion, ethnic origin
    6. control, consent
    7. personal, social
    8. potential
    9. stratification system

D. 1. wealth, power, prestige

2. caste, estate
3. SES index
4. 2,3
5. lower upper
6. one-half, upper, middle, lower
7. globalization, layoffs, unemployment
8. 15, poverty line, average
9. relative, absolute
10. homeless, underclass, new, overclass
11. child rearing, education, values

E.   1. move up or down
2. American dream
3. movement, down, up, down
4. education
5. special talent
6. insignificant

ANSWERS TO MULTIPLE CHOICE QUESTIONS:

1. b
2. d
3. c
4. a
5. b
6. b
7. a
8. a
9. c
10. d
11. d
12. a
13. c
14. b
15. c
16. d

CHAPTER 9: *MINORITY STATUS*

AGE, GENDER, AND SEXUALITY

In this chapter, you will learn:

1. that people are also treated unequally on the basis of such ascribed characteristics as age, gender and sexuality;
2. that the United States is becoming a society with an increasing proportion of elderly people;
3. of the existence and meaning of ageism;
4. that women are treated unequally;
5. how we acquire gender roles;
6. why sexism is an ideology detrimental to both men and women;
7. that sexual orientation is also subject to differential treatment.

TOPICAL OUTLINE

I. THE AGING SOCIETY
    A. Ageism
    B. Age Stratification
    C. Health
    D. Work and Retirement
    E. Finances
    F. Relationships with Others
    G. Widowhood
    H. Death and Dying

II. WOMEN: DIFFERENTIATION ACCORDING TO GENDER
    A. Biological Facts
        1. Differences: Nature
    B. Cultural Differences: Nurture
    C. Sex and Gender Differentiated
    D. The Cultural Construction Of Gender
    E. Traditional Gender Roles
    F. Theories of Gender Role Development
        1. Structural Functionalist Theory
        2. Conflict Theory
        3. Feminist Theory
    G. Theories of Socialization
        1. The Social Learning Theory
        2. Cognitive Development Theory
        3. Identification Theory
    H. Agents of Gender Socialization

1. The Media

III. SEXUALITY
   1. Homosexual Behavior
   2. Explanatory Theories of Homosexuality
   3. Bisexuality

A. CHAPTER OVERVIEW

The elderly in the United States suffer from loss of **status, income**, and **prestige,** even though they are an **ever-increasing proportion of the population.** Because of the speed of technological change in modern industrial societies, many young persons are better informed and have more skills than the old, at least in certain areas. As a result, **the old are devalued**. In addition, the elderly suffer from **declining health and vigor** and so deviate from the ideal norms that prevail in a society that extols youth, beauty, and fitness. Many of the elderly add **financial difficulties** to their health problems; this is especially true of **elderly women** and members of **minority** groups. Discrimination against the elderly has been obvious in the area of **employment**, where the cards are stacked against anyone over age 40. In addition, many employers enforce a **retirement age of 65 or 70**, which forces some employees to disengage before they are ready. **Disengagement** is supposed to be a mutual process by which the elderly give up **social and occupational** roles **voluntarily** so that these roles may be filled by younger persons. Other theoretical frameworks within which the elderly are studied include the **modernization, interactionist, subculture, activity, exchange, and age stratification theories.**

A.   Fill in the Blanks
1. Discrimination of the elderly is based on their loss of _____, _____, and _____.
2. This is very shortsighted since they are a _____ segment of our population.
3. The reason for discriminating is that our culture favors _____.
4. The rapidity of technological progress causes the _____ to know more than the _____, who are then _____.
5. Financial difficulties and _____ _____ are particularly severe for _____ and _____.
6. Pressure to retire forces some elderly to _____ prematurely.
7. The elderly are studied by such theories as _____, _____, _____, activity, exchange, and age stratification.

B. CHAPTER OVERVIEW

Many of the **myths** about the elderly are patently **untrue**. **Not all** are **senile** or miserable or lonely; only a **minority** have serious **health problems**; they are **not all poor** nor do they all hate retirement. **Most** live **independent lives**. **Many** do face **widowhood** and the consequent loneliness of **bereavement**, and when their physical and mental health wanes, they may face **institutionalization**. None of these are pleasant conclusions to life; however, inasmuch as the elderly are a growing segment of society, it is likely that the negative attitudes toward them will be somehow reversed.

B. FILL IN THE BLANKS

1. Many of the beliefs about the elderly are _____.
2. Only a _____ are sick, poor, and dependent.
3. However, many eventually have to be _____.
4. Widowhood for many leads to _____ of bereavement.
In the future, _____ attitudes should be _____.

C. CHAPTER OVERVIEW

The fact that humanity exists in **two sexes** has brought it much conflict. In the war between the sexes, **women** appear to be the **losers**. From a biological point of view, the **two sexes are needed** in order for the species to **reproduce**: the function of males is to deposit sperm in the reproductive organs of females; the function of females is to carry the resulting embryo—and then the fetus—until it emerges as a fully formed human child. Both can then nurture it until it can exist independently. **Throughout history**, these different biological functions have **resulted** in societies treating the two sexes **differentially and unequally**. **Differences** between men and women are of an **anatomical, genetic, and hormonal nature**. These differences certainly have effects on the behavior of men and women. Some of these differences seem to indicate that **females** are **more social**, more **suggestible**, have **lower self-esteem**—at least beginning with adolescence—and are **less achievement oriented** than **males** who are judged to be **more aggressive, assertive**, and have more **analytical** minds. There is also evidence that females are **superior in verbal ability** and seem inclined to **nurture** infants and children, while **males** excel in **spatial** and **quantitative** abilities.   What remains **unclear** is whether these traits are **inborn** or a result of differences in **socialization** experiences.

C. FILL IN THE BLANKS

1. The human race exists in two _____, which has engendered much _____.

2. The biological function of males is to _____ females, and the function of females is to _____ _____ to the new generation.
3. The different biological functions of males and females have historically given rise to social _____ and _____.
4. Differences between males and females are of an _____, _____, and _____ nature.
5. The above differences have an important effect on the _____ of men and women.
6. Observations indicate that women are more _____, _____, have lower _____ _____, and are less _____ _____ than men.
7. Females have also superior _____ _____and more _____ toward infants and children.
8. Males seem to be more _____, _____, and have better _____ and _____abilities.
9. What has not been proven is whether these differences are _____ or _____.

D. CHAPTER OVERVIEW

Even though we all born either men or women, we must become **socialized** into **sex roles**. Such socialization begins in the cradle: girl and boy babies are treated differently. Researchers theorize that socialization into sex roles occurs in the context of the **functionalist** and **conflict theories** through such processes as **social learning**, the **cognitive developmental** model, and **identification.** As to the agents of socialization, they are still the **family**, the **peer** group, the **school**, and the **mass** media.

The fact that women have been **treated unequally** in most societies has had **consequences** on their lives. Traditional gender roles have been permeated by a **sexist ideology** that justifies the inequality between the sexes. The obvious **effect** of sexism is that many options have been closed to women who have been relegated for centuries to the roles of wives and mothers and little else. Sociocultural changes in contemporary postindustrial societies have opened more avenues for women. However, the entrance of so many women into the work force and the consequent displacement of marriage and family have left many women puzzled and confused. It remains difficult for many women to reconcile their aspirations for personal achievement with their desire for a traditional family life. As a result, both men's and women's gender   roles still remain far from clear-cut.

D. FILL IN THE BLANKS

1. Sex roles must be learned in the process of _____ even though we are born either one sex or the other.

2. Sex role learning occurs in the context of _____ and _____ theories through the processes of _____ _____, the _____ _____ model, and _____.

3. The principal agents of socialization include the _____, the ____ _____, the _____, and the _____ _____.

4. Traditional sex roles are governed by a _____ ideology.

5. Women have been treated _____ in all societies of the world.

6. The foremost result of sexism is that it has shut off _____ to women, relegating them to the roles of _____ and _____.

7. _____ change in _____ societies has opened up many new avenues to women.

8. However, the entrance of many women into the _____ _____ has had the effect of _____ marriage and family.

9. The attempt to reconcile _____ aspirations and the desire for a traditional _____ have left many women _____.

E. CHAPTER OVERVIEW

In acquiring a **sexual personality**, not everyone is drawn to **heterosexuality.** Some individuals are drawn to members of their **own gender**, becoming **homosexuals** and **lesbians**. Still others are attracted to **both sexes**, sometimes establishing a paired relationship with one gender after some experimentation, or otherwise remaining **bisexual** throughout their lives. Scientists have not established a definite cause for these behaviors.

E. FILL IN THE BLANKS

1. In acquiring sex roles, some individuals are attracted to others of the _____ ___.

2. Still other individuals are attracted to _____ sexes equally.

3. Paired relationships by _____ and _____ are becoming more common.

4. The reasons for _____ _____ attraction is still being _____.

Terms to Keep in Mind

activity theory In the study of the elderly, the theory that the key to successful aging is to replace former roles with new ones.

ageism An ideology which asserts the superiority of the young over the old. Used to justify discrimination against the elderly in political, economic, and social areas.

anatomical differences: consist of the physical structure and appearance of the two sexes. The most important anatomical difference lies in the distinct reproductive systems of males and females.

androgyny: The possession in one personality of both male and female sex-typed traits and abilities.

cognitive development theory : according to this theory, children learn gender roles according to which stage of cognitive development they have reached at any point. Cognitive development is the way information is processed by individuals at different stages of physical
maturation.

conflict theory: another popular sociological theory which assumes that power and privilege are based on the resources that an individual possesses.

disengagement A theory of aging which posits that the elderly withdraw from their former social and occupational roles so that these may be filled by the young. This should occur by mutual consent.

exchange theory In the study of the elderly, the theory that the disadvantaged position of the elderly in American society is due to their lack of the social and material resources that would make them valuable in interactions with the young.

expressive role: emphasizes nurturing, emotion, and peacemaking.

feminist theory: this theory has borrowed much of the framework of conflict theory, especially the fact that women are underrepresented in positions of power in the society at large, a reflection of the lack of power women have within the family.

gender: Psychological characteristics that develop when an individual is assigned to either the male or female sex. Expressed in terms of the adjectives "masculine" and "feminine" as opposed to genetically determined sex, which is expressed in terms of "male" and "female."

gender roles: traditionally, the **instrumental** role is assigned to males and the **expressive** role is assigned to females

hormones : chemicals that are secreted into the bloodstream by glands located in the body with the function of stimulating some chemical processes and inhibiting others.

instrumental role: stresses rationality, competitiveness, aggression, and goal-orientation.

interactionist theory In the study of the elderly, a theory that focuses on the shared meanings that the elderly hold in common.

male or female: **biological** terms, descriptive of biological facts. They refer to a **sex status**, ascribed and not subject to change except in extraordinary circumstances.

masculine and feminine: reflect **social** conditions, describing how males and females are expected to behave in a given society, and how they come to feel about themselves. It is a

gender role, achieved and thus subject to change according to place and time.

modernization theory In the study of the elderly, the theory that the status of older people declines as the society in which they live becomes more modern and industrial

secondary sex characteristics: include height, weight, distribution of body fat and hair, and musculature.

sex chromosomes: contain the genes that determine heredity in all living creatures.

HOW MUCH DO YOU RECALL? TEST YOUR KNOWLEDGE
MULTIPLE CHOICE QUESTIONS

1. Concerning sex roles, it may be concluded that to a certain extent they differ because:
   a. men and nurturing women have different personalities
   b. women are because of their reproductive functions
   c. men are aggressive because they have to protect women
   d. males and females are treated and taught differently, thus developing different sex roles

2. Biological differences between men and women include:
   a. anatomical difference
   b. hormonal differences
   c. genetic differences
   d. all of the above

3. Which statement is false?
   a. All elderly are less productive than young people.
   b. Age differentiation is characteristic of industrial societies.
   c. A definite retirement age is a benefit the elderly have been working for.
   d. all of the above.

4. The most distinctive anatomical difference between men and women lies in:
   a. height
   b. weight
   c. reproductive systems
   e. hormones

5. Hormones are:
   a. toxic plants found in Latin America

b. chemicals secreted into the bloodstream by glands located in the body
c. found in food and drink with a wheat base
   man-made materials used in the making of perfume

6. It is through symbolic interaction that:
   a. individuals begin to label people and behavior as masculine or feminine
   b. people develop mental illness
   c. children decide to run away from home
   d. people learn how to make money

7. Androgyny refers to:
   a. a movement of gay men and women
   b. the existence in one personality of both male and female traits
   c. being a transvestite
   d. fulfilling the roles of the opposite sex

8. The process that elderly people undergo when they willingly withdraw from many of their previous interactions and occupational roles is called:
   a. disengagement
   b. rejuvenation
   c. corruption
   d. self-denial

9. The process of growing old is known as:
   a. deterioration
   b. altercation
   c. senescence
   d. effervescence

10. Among humans, sex is:
    a. an instinct
    b. a drive
    c. an institution
    d. all of the above

11. Steven Golden's crosscultural research indicates:
    a. matriarchal societies occur as frequently as patriarchal ones
    b. patriarchy is a universal characteristic of societies
    c. women often dominate male-female relationships
    d. none of the above

12. Gender socialization takes place through:
a. conditioning
b. identification or modelling
c. self definition
d. all of the above

13. The double standard refers to:
a. equal pay for equal work
b. quota systems
c. norms regarding the sexual conduct of males and females
d. all of the above

14. Ageism asserts that:
a. wisdom accompanies advancing age
b. each stage of life has its own rewards
c. the young are superior to the old
d. life begins at forty

15. More than 40 percent of elderly women, as opposed to almost 74 percent of
    elderly men, live with their spouses because:
a. women choose to divorce once their husbands retire
b. men do not like to live alone
c. women tend live longer than men
d. men are more likely to have Alzheimer's disease

16. The Age Discrimination Act of 1967:
a. does not include elderly workers
b. prohibits employers to fire anyone over 60
c. prohibits employers to force retirement before age 70
d. protects the over-80 age cohort

17. Secondary sex characteristics are chiefly determined by:
a. hormones
b. the environment
c. chromosomal structure
d. symbolic interaction

18. Femininity and masculinity are:
a. biological terms
b. cultural concepts
c. subcultures in the wider society
d. equivalent to sex and gender

19. Homosexual behavior:
a. is an effect of the loose morals of this century
b. is against God and nature
c. has been sanctioned in all societies
d. has been known to exist throughout history

20. Bisexuality:
a. is explained in the same way by men and women
b. represents another plague of the 20th century
c. is rationalized by men as the need for sexual variety
d. is explained by women as the need to take revenge on men

ANSWERS TO FILL IN THE BLANKS:

A.
1. status, prestige, income
2. growing
3. youth
4. young, elderly, devalued
5. health problems, women, minorities
6. disengage
7. modernization, interactionist, subculture

B.
1. untrue
2. minority
3. institutionalized
4. loneliness
5. negative, reversed

C.
1. sexes, conflicts
2. impregnate, give birth
3. differentiation inequality
4. anatomical, hormonal, genetic
5. behavior
6. social, suggestible, self-esteem, achievement-oriented
7. verbal ability, nurturant
8. aggressive, assertive, analytical quantitative

D.
1. socialization
2. social learning, cognitive developmental, identification
3. family, peer group, school

4. sexist
5. unequally
6. options, wives, mothers
7. sociocultural, postindustrial
8. workforce, displacing
9. professional family, confused

E.
1. same sex
2. both
3. gays, lesbians
4. same-sex, debated

ANSWERS TO MULTIPLE CHOICE QUESTIONS:

1. d
2. d
3. d
4. c
5. b
6. a
7. c
8. b
9. c
10. b
11. b
12. d
13. c
14. c
15. c
16. c
17. a
18. b
19. d
20. c

CHAPTER 10: FROM THE PLOW TO THE COMPUTER

CHANGE, COLLECTIVE BEHAVIOR, AND SOCIAL MOVEMENTS

In this chapter, you will learn

1. that change is a constant feature of life, but the speed of change has become more rapid in the modern world;

2. that change may be viewed from several perspectives: as modernization, as the consequence of war and conquest, or as the result of a world system;

3. some of the sources of change;

4. the processes of social and cultural change;

5. the relationship of technology to change;

6. the meaning of collective behavior, where and why it occurs;

7. the definition, and kinds of, crowds, panics, mobs, riots, and mass hysteria;

8. the nature of publics and public opinion;

9. about social movements, their traits and characteristics;

10. about some of the causes of social movements.

TOPICAL OUTLINE

I. SOCIETY AND CHANGE
   A. Levels of Change

II. PROCESSES OF SOCIAL AND CULTURAL CHANGE
   A. Social Change
       1. Planning
       2. Reform
       3. Revolution
   B. Cultural Change
       1. Innovation
       2. Discovery
       3. Diffusion

III. THE SOURCES OF CHANGE
   A. The Physical Environment
       1. Geography
       2. Population
   B. Ideas or Belief Systems
       1. Social Movements
       2. War and Conquest
   C. Random Events

IV. TECHNOLOGY
    A. Results of the First Technological Revolution

V. THE INDUSTRIAL REVOLUTION
    A. Inventions and Discoveries of the Industrial Revolution
        1. automation
        2. mechanization

VI. INDUSTRIALISM
    A. The Factory

VII. TECHNOLOGY AND SOCIAL CHANGE
    A. Modernization

VIII. COLLECTIVE BEHAVIOR
    A. Crowds
        1. casual
        2. organized
        3. expressive
        4. acting
    B. Mobs and Riots
        1. Rumors
        2. Fashions, Fads, and Crazes
        3. Panics and Mass Hysteria

IX. PUBLICS AND PUBLIC OPINION
    A. Public Opinion
        1. The Formation of Public Opinion
        2. The Mass Media
    B. Measuring Public Opinion
        1. Sampling
        2. Interpretation
    C. Propaganda and Censorship

X. SOCIAL MOVEMENTS
    A. Types of Social Movements
        1. Reform
        2. Revolutionary
            a. nationalistic
            b. class
            c. Factors encouraging revolutionary movements
        3. Change-resistant
    B. Stages in Social Movements
        1. Emergence

　　　　2. Coalescence
　　　　3. Bureaucratization
　　　　4. Decline
　　C. Conditions for the Rise of Social Movements
　　　　1. relative deprivation
　　　　2. failure of rising expectations

A. CHAPTER OVERVIEW

Change is an integral part of nature and of all living things, although a degree of **stability** is equally characteristic of individuals, societies, and cultures. The **mechanisms** of sociocultural **change** are easier to determine than its causes. The principal processes of cultural change are **discovery, invention, and diffusion**. On the other hand, **change in the structure of society**--or social change--occurs through **planning, reform, and revolution.** Sources of change include the **physical environment**, the **size and structure of populations, ideology, events** and individuals, and **technology.**

Sociocultural change has been triggered chiefly by **technological progress. Technology** includes all the **methods** and **devices** that help humans manage and **control** their **environment.** The **first** technological **breakthrough** was the invention of agriculture. A **second** was the advent of the **machine era**, or the **Industrial Revolution.** Although this movement accelerated in the middle of the eighteenth century in Great Britain, its roots go back several centuries. Its effects are still being felt by the world. The most **significant** changes brought about by the Industrial Revolution are a surge in the growth of **population; industrialization,** or the dependence of the economy on industry; and **urbanization**, or the growth of cities at the expense of rural life.

A. FILL IN THE BLANKS:

1. The most dominant element in the universe is _____.
2. An equally common characteristic of individuals and societies, however, is

   _____.
3. The causes of sociocultural change are _____ to establish.
4. The processes of change are _____ to determine: they are _____,
   _____, and _____.
5. Social change, on the other hand, occurs through _____, _____,
   and _____.
6. The sources of change include the physical environment, _____,
   _____, _____, and _____.
7. Technological progress has been triggered primarily by _____ change.
8. Technology includes all the methods and devices that help humans
   _____ their environment.

9. The first technological breakthrough was the invention of _____.
10. The second technological breakthrough was the _____ _____.
11. The most significant effects of the Industrial Revolution are the growth of _____, _____, and _____.

B. CHAPTER OUTLINE

Change in society results in **modernization**, an all-embracing process that involves primarily the change from a **preindustrial** to an **industrial** mode of production, but affects all areas of human life, not only the economic. The **technologically-advanced** nations are already modernized and are said to be entering a **postindustrial** era. The less developed nations are trying to catch up as they see the high standard of living that industrialization has brought.

Modernization is not achieved without sacrifice. A totally **new system of production** is **superimposed** on a society that has survived at a subsistence level. In the process, many **traditions** and an entrenched way of life are **destroyed**. The social organization of societies is altered and a **new** type of **social organization** supersedes it. In Britain, for instance, farmers and serfs became industrial workers, moved to cities from farms, began to work in exchange for wages, accepted a secondary relationship with their employers, and started living in nuclear families. These **changes** resulted in **new values**, new **political** and **economic systems**, and even new personalities emerging. When **change** proceeds **slowly**, integration into the existing order, though difficult, eventually succeeds, and **accommodation** takes place. But when the change is **fast**, modernization brings with it **dislocations** and strains that evidence themselves in feelings of **rootlessness, anomie,** and sometimes **violence**. Such has been the case in the colonized nations that have been trying to modernize their economies as rapidly as possible, creating in this way conflicts with the established forces of tradition. The **political instability** in these newly-independent societies often results in **military dictatorships**, **millenarian religions**, **revolutionary** movements, and extreme **nationalism**.

B. FILL IN THE BLANKS:

1. Modernization is the consequence of _____.
2. Modernization involves primarily the change from a _____to an _____mode of production, but affects_____ _____of human life.
3. The technologically-advanced societies are entering a_____ era.
4. With modernization, a totally new _____ must be superimposed on a society that has survived at a_____ level.

5. The process of modernization destroys many _____ and an entrenched ___ ___ _____.
6. In the example of Britain, people had to move to _____, become _____ workers, accept _____ for their work, enter into a _____-_____ relationship with employers, and live in a _____ family.
7. Modernization results in new _____, new economic and political _____, and new _____ emerging.
8. When change is slow, _____ into the existing order takes place.
9. When change is rapid, _____ and _____ result, leading to _____, _____, and even violence.
10. As a result, nations so affected are politically _____.

C. CHAPTER OUTLINE

Technology is also the practical application of knowledge; thus, it builds upon existing knowledge and technology. The more technologically advanced a society is, the more rapid is technological progress. **Modern industrial societies** are characterized by the **most rapid rates of change** ever known so that each generation's experience is unique. Technology has radically **altered human lives**; it is so important that some social thinkers believe that it determines society's culture (**technological determinism**). Moreover, it is thought that change occurs first in the **material culture**, and only later do values, ideas, and norms follow. Thus there is always a **culture lag** which produces **social problems** and disorganization (William Ogburn's cultural lag theory). However, change does not occur in isolation but in the context of a number of social phenomena; thus it has no **single** cause.

C. FILL IN THE BLANKS:

1. Technology builds upon existing _____.
2. Modern industrial societies are characterized by the most _____ change.
3. Technology has radically altered _____ _____.
4. According to technological determinism, technology determines a society's _____.
5. Change occurs first in _____ _____.
6. The cultural lag theory was the work of _____ _____.
7. A culture lag generally produces _____ _____
8. Change has no single _____.

D. CHAPTER OUTLINE

Some social thinkers have concluded that the end product of social change, through modernization, is a **trend** toward **mass society**. A mass society is one that evidences a degree of **social disorganization** and is characterized by a **loosely** integrated social organization. A mass society need not be large in numbers, but it is **composed** of **masses of people** who are widely distributed and **anonymous** in the sense that they may react to the same stimuli, but have no reference to one another.

Mass society represents the **end** of the continuum from Gemeinschaft to Gesellschaft societies (See Chapter 4). It is the **last stage** in the transition from **primary to secondary** relationships. It is characterized by **high mobility**, **anonymity**, **specialization of roles** and statuses, and a **lack** in the ability of individuals to **integrate** themselves into the social system--more people feel that they do not fit in. They make choices without regard to customs, traditions, norms, and values.

The tendency toward mass society is reinforced by a system of **mass communication**. Communication is essential to all culture building, but with the present technology the **same message** is transmitted to **millions of people simultaneously**. Such direct and rapid communication has dramatically changed the old social structure of societies.

D. FILL IN THE BLANKS:

1. The end product of sociocultural change, through modernization, is the trend toward a _____ _____ .
2. A mass society evidences a degree of _____ and is characterized by a loosely _____social order.
3. A mass society is composed of masses of people who are widely _____and _____ .
4. Mass society represents the end of the _____from Gemeinschaft to _____ .
5. Mass society is the last stage in the transition from _____to _____relationships.
6. Mass society is characterized by_____ _____,_____, specialization of _____, and lack of _____ability.

E. CHAPTER OUTLINE

The **danger** in a mass society is that the masses can easily by **mobilized** and led by an **organized elite**, which is a threat to democracy.

Masses engage in the kind of behavior that social scientists call collective and that tends to be **unorganized, unstructured,** and **uncoordinated** but also very **susceptible** to action, including violent action, especially under the direction of a charismatic leader.

Technologically advanced societies are more often subject to various forms of collective behavior than traditional societies. **Collective behavior occurs** in situations that are highly charged with **emotion** and in which the usual norms do not apply. Such situations include **crowds (riots, mobs, panics), rumors, fashions, fads, crazes, publics and audiences, public opinion, propaganda and censorship, and social movements**.

Collective behavior occurs most often in **crowd** situations. A crowd is a temporary collection of people who respond to the same stimulus. There are **casual** crowds (people waiting at a red light), **organized** crowds (a concert or football game), **expressive** crowds (a protest rally or religious revival meeting), and **acting** crowds (mob, riots, violent protest meetings). Any crowd can become a **panic** crowd, a **mob**, or a **riot** if the right stimuli are present, but an organized crowd is particularly receptive to mob behavior.

People in crowds tend to develop a **common mood**; ideas of what constitutes acceptable behavior emerge at the moment, and the behavior may be of an antisocial nature. A crowd **lacks norms** and is removed from social control. In addition, individuals shed their identity and **act as a group**. This absolves individuals of any guilt for the actions of the group. Nonetheless, a **crowd seldom** does anything beyond what individuals would do; and its **violence is directed** against a definite target.

Publics--scattered collections of people who **temporarily share** a common interest or concern about an issue--are also a form of collective behavior. The large number of publics in advanced societies generates **public opinion**, which is the **attitude** or judgment **of a large number of people** on a specific issue. Public opinion is especially important in **democratic societies** and is greatly influenced by the mass media. The latter sometimes use propaganda and/or censorship to manipulate public opinion. **Propaganda** is a deliberate **attempt to persuade** people to accept a belief uncritically or to make a specific choice. **Censorship distorts information** by suppressing or deleting parts or all of it.

E. FILL IN THE BLANKS:

1. Collective behavior takes place without _____ direction from the_____ _____of society.
2. Additional characteristics of collective behavior are:
it is: _____,_____,_____, and

_____.
3. Collective behavior is prevalent during times of _____ _____

_____.

4. A crowd is a _____ collection of people who respond to the same _____.
5. Crowds may be _____, _____, _____, and _____.
6. In a crowd, people develop a_____ _____, shed their _____, and create new _____ of acceptable behavior.
7. Although a crowd acts as a group, absolving individuals of any _____, the crowd will not go beyond what any individual would _____and its violence is directed against a definite _____.
8. Additional forms of collective behavior include _____, _____, _____, _____, and _____opinion.

9. A public is a scattered _____of people who _____a common interest or are _____by a common event.
10. The element holding a public together is _____.
11. Publics are _____, _____, and their _____ changes rapidly.
12. Publics are more characteristic of _____than of _____societies.
13. Publics give rise to_____ _____.
14. The dominant opinion of a large public is_____ _____.
15. Public opinion is less important in _____societies because _____issues seldom arise.
16. Certain groups in society manipulate public opinion through _____and _____.
17. Propaganda gives a _____interpretation to an issue.
18. Censorship _____information altogether.

F. CHAPTER OVERVIEW

Social movements consist of **collective behavior** that has as its goal the **alteration** of some aspect of the **social system**. During periods of rapid social change, people look for a **systematic** way of **interpreting** emerging perspectives. At such times, they are **receptive to ideologies**, which are systems of beliefs (doctrines) providing a basis for collective action. Ideologies **explain** why things are as they are; they **reinforce** the feelings of believers; and **direct** believers to action that will result in social change. Unfortunately, ideologies sometimes **distort** facts, and make their followers "true believers" blindly loyal to them.

Conditions that promote the **rise** of social movements include: **rapid social change**; feelings of **alienation** or normlessness on the part of individuals resulting from the unresponsiveness of the existing social structures; **relative**

deprivation, that is, a desire on the part of some groups for the advantages enjoyed by other groups; **rising expectations**, or the fact that, having achieved some benefits, further aspirations are being blocked by existing social structures; and **downward mobility**, or loss of former status and wealth.

The two social movements that have had the most influence on societies have been the **revolutionary** and the **reform** movements. Reform movements attempt to alter some aspect of the social structure without overturning the entire structure. Often they seek to correct parts of a system that has strayed from its original purpose. Revolutionary movements attempt to supplant an entire social system with a new one. In a **nationalistic** revolutionary movement, a predominantly foreign government is overthrown and replaced with a native one. In a **class** revolutionary movement, one ruling class is substituted for another. **Change-resistant** movements reflect the belief that change occurs too rapidly. These movements want to protect the status quo from reform movements.

F. FILL IN THE BLANKS:

1. Social movements are _____ of collective behavior with the goal of _____ some aspect of the social system.
2. In times of rapid social change, people are receptive to _____.
3. Systems of beliefs, or doctrines, are called _____.
4. The functions of ideologies include _____, _____, and _____ toward action.
5. Social movements that are successful become _____.
6. The characteristics of social movements include: they are_____, they involve _____ _____, and they are _____ at a specific goal.
7. Among the conditions that promote the rise of social movements are: rapid_____ _____, feelings of _____, relative _____ and rising _____.
8. The two social movements that have had the most influence on societies in recent times have been: the _____ and the _____.
9. Revolutionary movements may be _____ or _____ movements.
10. The movement that tries to protect the status quo from change perceived as too rapid is _____.

TERMS TO REMEMBER

alienation: A feeling of powerlessness and insecurity, of not belonging in society, producing boredom and meaninglessness. Alienation provides a fertile ground for social movements and is characteristic of people in mass society.

cultural change: Change in values, beliefs, and norms which may be brought about by scientific discoveries, technological inventions, new achievements in the arts, or shifts in religious doctrine.

cultural lag theory: The theory that different parts of a culture change at different rates of speed, creating dislocations and disorganization in the society. Associated with William Ogburn.

diffusion: A process of cultural change in which cultural traits are spread from one society to another (or from one group to another).

discovery: A process of cultural change in which an already existing fact or relationship is newly perceived.

invention: A process of cultural change in which old cultural ideas of existing objects are combined in new ways to produce ideas or objects more important than the previous ones had been separately.

mass communication: The relatively simultaneous exposure of large heterogeneous audiences to symbols transmitted by impersonal means from organized sources to whom audience members are anonymous.

mass society: The model (theoretical construct) of a society toward which postindustrial societies are drifting. It consists of an undifferentiated mass of people and an elite capable of dominating and manipulating it. It is highly urbanized and industrialized and displays secondary relationships, lack of traditional values, alienation, anomie, pressure to conform, and subjection to manipulation through the mass media.

modernization: Sociocultural change that transforms small preindustrial societies into large industrial ones.

social change: Change in the patterns of social interaction in which a substantial number of society's members assume new statuses and play new roles. Takes place through planning, reform, or revolution.

technology: All the methods and devices that help humans manage and control their environment.

HOW MUCH DO YOU REMEMBER? TEST YOUR KNOWLEDGE

MULTIPLE CHOICE QUESTIONS

1. Which is **not** one of the revolutionary changes that have transformed Western societies?
   a. The substitution of agrarian economies with industrial ones
   b. Dramatic increases in population
   c. The enduring role of religion
   d. Urbanization and bureaucratization

2. Which is **false** of social change?
   a. It occurs when some members of society assume new statuses and fill new roles
   b. It occurs through planning, reform, or revolution
   c. It must take place in material culture first
   d. All of the above

3. Cultural change:
   a. cannot exist separately and distinctly from social change
   b. occurs as a result of revolutionary changes of government
   c. refers to change in the patterns of interaction among individuals and groups
   d. is an invention of social scientists

4. Which is an example of cultural change?
   a. Fidel Castro's takeover in Cuba
   b. The Social Security Act
   c. The automobile
   d. Zoning laws changing residential patterns

5. Which is an example of social change?
   a. The discovery of electricity
   b. The Cultural Revolution in China in which the roles of peasants and middle-class persons were somewhat reversed
   c. The use of steam to power machinery
   d. The sexual revolution

6. When existing knowledge is put to new use it is termed:
   a. diffusion
   b. innovation
   c. invention
   d. discovery

7. All the methods, devices, and human-made artifacts that help people manage and control their environment are called:
    a. automation
    b. technology
    c. instruments
    d. tools

8. Which was **not** an effect of the Industrial Revolution?
    a. The mechanization of agriculture and manufacturing
    b. The application of power to manufacturing
    c. A reversal to older systems of economics
    d. The movement of people from rural areas to cities

9. The production process became more efficient when:
    a. apprentices were hired instead of families
    b. machinery was installed in English cottages
    c. craftsmen began putting out their products for sale
    d. workers were housed in factories and a bureaucratic system emerged

10. Mass communication today is:
    a. public
    b. rapid
    c. outside of normal interaction
    d. all of the above

11. Change experienced on a middle level includes:
    a. the breakup of many nuclear families
    b. urbanization
    c. the incorporation of previously excluded groups within the political process
    d. the proliferation of career choices for individuals

12. Sociocultural change refers to:
    a. changes in norms, values, material objects
    b. reforms to laws and institutions
    c. the creation of new roles and statuses
    d. all of the above

13. According to Daniel Bell, the third technological revolution consists of the:
    a. joining of computers with telecommunications
    b. development of petrochemicals and synthetics
    c. applications of steam power to manufacturing
    advent of telephones

14. Collective behavior is often precipitated by:
    a. anomaly
    b. rapid social change
    c. deviant behavior
    d. fear of the future

15. Which is **not** a characteristic of crowd behavior?
    a. Individuals maintain their identity
    b. Development of a common mood
    c. Behavior according to previously established norms
    d. Temporary

16. A scattered collection of people who share a common interest or a concern about an issue is a(n):
    a. group
    b. crowd
    c. public
    e. audience

17. Attempts to persuade the individual to accept a particular belief, or to make a specific choice, uncritically, include:
    a. public relations and advertising
    b. sales, sales promotion, and political campaigns
    c. propaganda
    d. all of the above

18. Which is **not** a form of collective behavior?
    a. Fashions
    b. Rumors
    c. Dining out with a friend
    d. Panic

19. A temporary collection of people gathered in the same place at the same time becomes a crowd when they:
    a. interact on a face-to-face basis
    b. respond to a common stimulus
    c. are personally acquainted with each other
    d. have the same thing in mind as to how to behave

20. Which is **NOT** an element of a social movement?
    a. It has a specific perspective and ideology
    b. It involves no orientation toward action
    c. It has a strong sense of idealism and solidarity
    d. It involves a significant number of people

21. Collective behavior is:
   a. rather unstructured
   b. well planned
   c. based on regular norms
   d. individual behavior multiplied

22.   Many listeners to a 1938 science-fiction radio program believe that Martians were really invading the Earth. They fled into the streets in panic. We would call their behavior
   a. fashion
   b. rational-legal behavior
   c. fantasy
   d. none of the above
   e. all of the above

23. Violent crowd behavior:
   a. has no limits in its antisocial nature
   b. always goes against the wishes of individual members
   c. is generally random
   d. is usually long-lasting

24. Censorship:
   a. is the same as propaganda
   b. gives a one-sided interpretation of an issue
   c. deletes all or parts of information
   d. the opposite of propaganda

ANSWERS TO FILL IN THE BLANKS

A. 1. change
   2. stability
   3. difficult
   4. easier; discovery, invention, and diffusion
   5. planning, reform, revolution
   6. population, ideology, events, and technology
   7. sociocultural
   8. control
   9. agriculture
   10. Industrial Revolution
   11. Population, industrialization, urbanization

B. 1. Change

2. preindustrial, industrial, all areas
3. postindustrial
4. system of production, subsistence
5. traditions, way of life
6. cities, industrial, wages, secondary, nuclear
7. values, systems, personalities
8. integration
9. dislocation, strain, rootlessness, anomie
10. unstable

C.　1. Knowledge
　　2. rapid
　　3. human life
　　4. culture
　　5. material culture
　　6. William Ogburn
　　7. Social problems
　　8. Cause

D. 1. Mass society
　2. social disorganization, integrated
　3. distributed, anonymous
　4. continuum, Gesellschaft
　5. primary, secondary
　6. high mobility, anonymity, roles and sta6tuses, integrative
　7. led, elite
　8. collective behavior, violent
　9. reached

E. 1. Clear-cut, normative system
　2. spontaneous, unpredictable, unstructured, unplanned
　3. rapid social change
　4. temporary, stimulus
　5. casual, organized, expressive, acting
　6. common mood, identity, norms
　7. guilt, do target
　8. rumors, fads, fashions, crazes, publics, public opinion
　9. collection, share, affected
　10. intellect
　11. temporary, dispersed, composition
　12. complex (heterogeneous), traditional
　13. public opinion

14. public opinion
15. traditional, conflicting
16. propaganda, censorship
17. one-sided
18. deletes

ANSWERS TO MULTIPLE CHOICE QUESTIONS

1. c
2. c
3. a
4. c
5. b
6. c
7. b
8. c
9. d
10. d
11. c
12. d
13. a
14. b
15. a
16. c
17. d
18. c
19. b
20. b
21. a
22. e
23. c
24. c

CHAPTER 11:

POPULATION, URBANIZATION, AND ENVIRONMENT

In this chapter, you will learn

1. the importance of the discipline of demography and its various concepts;
2. about the types of changes that occur within populations and their effects on societies;
3. of the dangers of overpopulation;
4. the meaning and effects of urbanization;
5. about the characteristics of American cities;
6. the difference between the process called urbanization and the attitude of urbanism, which has become predominant globally;
7. about the emergence of suburbanization and metropolitanization;
8. the nature of the urban crisis;
9. about the discipline of ecology;
10. that humans have damaging effects on the various ecosystems, including on the global ecosystem.

TOPICAL OUTLINE

I. POPULATION DENSITY
    A. Demographic Processes: Dynamics of Population Change
        1. Birthrates
        2. Fertility rate
        3. Fecundity rate
        4. Death Rates
        5. Migration
        6. Immigration
        7. Internal Migration

II. CHARACTERISTICS AND COMPOSITION OF A POPULATION
    A. Sex Ratio
    B. Age Structure
    C. Tomorrow's America

III. POPULATION AROUND THE WORLD
    A. Malthus and Marx

IV. DEMOGRAPHIC TRANSITION
    A. Zero Population Growth

A. CHAPTER OVERVIEW

One of the **side effects** of the Industrial Revolution which brought a higher standard of living to many societies has been the **growth of population.** Although overpopulation is said to be a problem that threatens future generations, it is differences in population **density** that are problematic-some regions are totally uninhabited, while others average tens of thousands of people per square mile. The statistical study of such characteristics as birthrates, death rates, sex ratios, age groups, marriage and divorce incidence, and human mobility are studied by the discipline of **demography.**

There are a variety of ways to **measure** population density, which is a **relative concept**--what is considered dense for a farming area may be sparse for an urban area. Demographers have devised the categories of densely settled, moderately settled, thinly settled, and largely unpopulated.

Another **important** demographic **concept** is that of **birthrates** which are the number of births per 1000 people in one given year. **Fertility rates** are the annual number of births per l000 women of child-bearing age (15-44). **High birthrates** seem to occur in the **less industrialized and urbanized countries**, whereas highly industrialized and urbanized nations tend to have the lowest birthrates. **Death, or mortality, rates** are the number of deaths per l000 people in a year. Death rates are **highest in tropical Africa and lowest in urban industrial nations.**

A. FILL IN THE BLANKS:

1. The growth of population has followed the improvement in the _____of _____resulting from the_____ _____.
2. Demography studies such subjects as _____, _____ _____, ____ _____,___ _____, _____incidence, and____ _____.
3. The crisis in population crisis is really the fact that_____ varies from very low to incredibly high.
4. Birthrates are the number of _____per _____women in any one _____.

5. The less industrialized and urbanized nations exhibit _____ birthrates, and vice versa.

B. CHAPTER OVERVIEW

The **population crisis** refers to the fact that the number of people in the world has been increasing geometrically (doubling) at ever shorter intervals of time. World population **doubles every 35 years**, so that every year there are about 75 million more births than deaths. Thomas **Malthus** predicted that this would happen and that the food supply would increase only in **arithmetic** progression, so that eventually it would be exhausted, which would cause starvation. Great advances in technology, agriculture, and methods of birth control have tempered this prophecy, but it remains relevant in the developing nations. In the Western world, population growth was accompanied by an increase in the standard of living. In the past 200 years, the Western world has undergone a **demographic transition**, that is, from high mortality and fertility rates to **low mortality** and **fertility** rates. Demographers believe that this pattern will be repeated in other regions.

The United States has attained **zero population growth** as of 1972 (the fertility rates dropped below the replacement level). American women now have l.8 children; but this rate is likely to increase with changed circumstances. The human race is multiplying at a **very rapid rate**, and the most rapid expansion of population is occurring in **poor, underdeveloped nations**. Tensions produced by conditions in these nations may lead to conflicts on a world level.

B. FILL IN THE BLANKS

1. World population doubles every _____ years.
2. Thomas Malthus predicted that food would grow in_____ progression.
3. The demographic transition has occurred in the_____ world where _____ fertility and mortality rates have declined.
4. In 1972, the United States reached _____ _____ _____ .

C. CHAPTER OVERVIEW

Although technology has provided effective means of birth control, lowering a population's birthrate is a **cultural**, and not only a technical matter. People have to become convinced that it is to their advantage to have smaller families, and they tend to do it in **urban environments** with industrial modes of production.

Food and population growth are highly related; on a world level, food production has grown faster than population of late. But **food production** is **not equally shared**. More than half of the food was consumed by the richest 30 percent of the world's people. Resources needed to support the Western lifestyle are **finite** and in danger of **depletion**; thus, it is prudent to plan to preserve them.

A final demographic concept is that of **age and sex distribution**, referring to the fact that populations vary not only in size but in age and sex, and that such inequalities have great **cultural** meanings for societies. A **graphic device** that indicates age distribution is the **population pyramid** which allows experts to predict population trends. In the United States the **median age** will continue to **increase** sharply over the next three decades; there are 6 million more females than males; whites have the highest median age; and the number of children under 5 has been shrinking.

C. FILL IN THE BLANKS

1. Lowering a nation's birthrate is a _____ as well as a _____ matter.
2. Populations vary not only in _____ but also in _____ and _____ .
3. A _____ _____ allows experts to predict population trends.

4. In the United States, the _____ _____will continue to   increase sharply over the next _____decades.

D. CHAPTER OVERVIEW

Urbanization is the **population trend** in which people **leave rural areas** to live in areas with a concentration of industry, business, and labor. The trend is the consequence of the fact that industry requires many workers, whereas mechanized agriculture requires fewer workers. Cities grew also as a result of **lower death rates**, **rising birth rates, and immigration**. The U.S. Bureau of the Census defines a city as an area with a population of at least 2500. Sociologists define the **ecological** city as an area composed of a **central city** with areas around it that are **economically and culturally** dependent on it. The movement of population in the United States has been from rural to urban to suburban areas. Only now is there evidence of a countertrend in that rural areas and small towns appear to be growing faster than cities.

Urbanization is an **ongoing** process. **Urbanism**, on the other hand, is a **condition** that includes a **set of attitudes**, and a quality of life distinct from the rural. Through mass communication, urbanism is being spread into all areas and is becoming a way of life for all. Consequently, it is destroying traditional rural values that revolved around primary relationships, historical continuity, and emotional involvement. These **traditional values** have been **idealized**: researchers found that small-town values are illusory, and that corruption and urban technology are rampant. Still, rural life is different from **urban life**. The latter is **characterized** by a **density** of physical structures, by the substitution of the **nuclear family** for the extended family, by **secondary** relationships, by a **lack of group identity**, by a **freedom** from constraints because of anonymity, and by a resulting **increase** in **formal controls**--laws, codes, and regulations.

The transformation of American cities began with the trend toward **suburban** living. Suburbs now house more people than central cities, offering such advantages as more green spaces, larger homes, less pollution, and greater safety. Suburbs have themselves become commercial, industrial, and recreational centers to the point of being **economically self sufficient**. The suburban trend has removed an important tax base from cities, forcing them to curtail many services, with the result that additional suburban migration occurs. Such a movement has left the lower socioeconomic groups as the primary residents of inner cities. Because suburbs are so prevalent, the Bureau of the Census uses SMSAs (**Standard Metropolitan Statistical Areas**) to measure units of population. A SMSA is an **area** consisting of one or two **central cities, suburbs, and small satellite municipalities**. In locations where one SMSA is joined to another without interruption, the condition is called **urban sprawl**, or

megalopolis, which has negative aspects in that it drains off resources of the city and creates conflicts among the large numbers of local governments.

The **urban crisis** has been intensified by the **move** of the middle class and industry to the **suburbs**. Inner cities overwhelmingly contain slums and/or ghettos from which the deprived and the trapped have little opportunity to leave. Cities, however, tend to have more **vitality** than suburbs because of the more varied group of people who inhabit them. Herbert **Gans** categorized urban dwellers as cosmopolites, the unmarried or childless, the ethnic villagers, the deprived, and the trapped. The first two categories are responsible for a trend toward **gentrification**, or an attempt to refurbish the decaying homes and neighborhoods. This trend may succeed where **urban renewal**, funded and administered by the government, has so far failed.

D. FILL IN THE BLANKS

1. _____ is the shift in population from rural to urban areas.
2. Central city degeneration and urban crisis result, at least partially, from the trend toward _____.
3. Additional reasons for the growth of cities are_____ ____ _____,_____
   _____, and _____.
4. A city, as defined by the U. S. Bureau of the Census, has at least
   _____inhabitants.
5. Urbanism is a _____that includes a set of_____
   and a_____ of _____distinct from the rural.
6. Urbanism is replacing traditional _____values that include _____
   _____,_____ _____, and_____ _____.
7. The most important trend, one that has created a crisis situation for the cities, has been _____.
8. The U. S. Bureau of the Census measures population units in terms of
   _____, and an uninterrupted string of them is called
   _____.
9. Inner cities invariably contain _____and _____
   which house those who have no _____to leave.
10. _____may succeed where _____
   has failed.

E. CHAPTER OUTLINE

Populations are analyzed within the framework of their natural environment. The **natural environment** is the total **complex** of natural conditions and resources that **characterizes** a specific area. It consists of such elements as **landforms**, **climate**, natural **vegetation, soils**, native **animal life**, underground and surface **waters**, and mineral **resources**. These elements change in time and location.

There is a **reciprocal relationship** between the environment and people and their cultures. The environment affects people's lives, and in turn it is affected by them, often in a negative way. However, the relationship is not simple and direct. People can live differently in similar environments, and differently at different times in the same environment. The **same environment** is **perceived** differently by different people at different times.

E. FILL IN THE BLANKS

1. The natural environment is the total complex of_____ _____ and
   _____that characterizes specific areas.
2. It consists of _____ _____, _____, _____, _____, _____,
   _____and _____.
3. There is a _____relationship between the natural environment and
   _____and their cultures.
4. This relationship is not_____ and _____.
5. The same environment may be _____and _____differently at
   different times and by different people.
6. The environment is radically altered by _____
   _____.
7. Changes in environment also affect _____.
8. The ecological crisis is not caused by _____ or
   _____ _____alone.

F. CHAPTER OUTLINE

The technology spawned by the **Industrial Revolution**, in spite of the many benefits it brought humanity, is now **endangering human life** on earth, according to some scientists. Part of the problem is our notion that we are in control of the world and need not worry about what we do to our ecosystem. The **ecosystem** is the **way living things interact** and interrelate among each other and their environment. This interaction maintains a **balance** that permits life to continue. People, land, animals, vegetation, atmosphere, and social processes are so interdependent that slight alterations in one affect all others. Ecosystems may be **local** (a lake), **regional** (an ocean), and **global** (the planet Earth). The **harmony** of the various ecosystems has been disturbed by environmental **pollution**, environmental **depletion**, and **overpopulation**.

Pollution is the result of human tampering with the environment that has harmful consequences. **Pollutants** are sometimes unforeseen and unwanted **byproducts** of human activities. **Air** pollution is caused by the **burning of fossil fuels** such as oil, natural gas, and coal. It has taken the form of **acid rain** and threats to the ozone layer. The first kills off some fish in lakes and rivers, and damages buildings; the second may result in a change of climate, the destruction of animal and plant life, a greater incidence of skin cancer and damage of a genetic nature, and reduced crop yields. **Water** pollution results from **oil spills** and dumping of wastes as well as from organic sewage, the overfertilization of water by excess nutrients, organic and inorganic chemicals, and sediments from soil erosion, radioactive substances, and waste heat from power plants. Herbicides, pesticides, chemical wastes, radioactive fallout, and garbage contribute to land pollution. Finally, prolonged exposure to intense noise damages hearing and increases irritability, preventing sleep, while certain forms of pollution lead to the deterioration of buildings, paintings, and statues, inhibits visibility, produces noxious odors, and obscures scenic views.

Even more acute than pollution is the problem of **depletion** of natural resources. No nation in the world is completely self-sufficient because once a natural resource has been used up, it is gone forever. The United States has to import a number of minerals already. Of most concern is the **depletion of oil** because our consumption of energy has been rising rapidly since the turn of the century. **Electrical power** is also undergoing constant increases in demand. Some experts maintain that nuclear sources are our only hope for the future, but others point to the severe limitations these sources have.

The Environmental Protection Agency has been established to deal with problems of pollution and resource depletion, and the Clean Air Act empowered the EPA to clean up the atmosphere. But pressures from the business community in weak economic times make rigid control difficult. Ultimately our **cultural values** will have to be changed in order to make any significant difference.

F. FILL IN THE BLANKS

1. The ecosystem is the way living things_____ and _____to each other and to the environment.
2. The interaction within the ecosystem maintains a _____that allows life to _____.
3. Ecosystems are divided into _____, _____, and _____.
4. The harmony of the various ecosystems has been disturbed by _____ _____,_____ _____, and _____.
5. Pollution is the result of human _____with the environment that has _____results.
6. Air pollution is caused by the _____of _____ _____for energy.
7. Acid rain and threats to the ozone layer are forms of _____ _____.
8. Oil spills and dumping of waste products are forms of

_____ _____.

9. Even more acute than pollution is the problem of _____
_____.

10. Rigid control by the _____is difficult because of pressures from the_____ _____, especially in a weak economy.

TERMS TO REMEMBER

biosphere: A thin film of air, water, and soil surrounding the earth.

birthrates: The number of births per 1000 persons in a specific population per year.

death rates: The number of deaths per 1000 persons in a specific population per year. Same as mortality rate.

demography: The study of the growth or decline of populations,   their distribution throughout the world, and their composition.

ecology: The study of the relationship between living organisms and their environments.

ecosystem: The way living and nonliving entities interact and maintain a balance that permits life to continue.

fecundity: The biological potential for producing offspring.

fertility: The number of actual births per 1000 women between the ages of 15 and 44.

infant mortality: The rate that reflects the number of deaths among infants under one year of age for every 1000 live births.

life expectancy: The average number of years that a person at a given age can expect to live.

megalopolis: A complex in which one metropolitan area follows another without interruption. Also called urban sprawl.

metropolitanization: The tendency of suburbs, small cities, and surrounding rural areas to cluster around a central city and be considered as a single unit.

mortality rates: The number of deaths in a population per year.

pollution: The degradation of air, land, and water as well as the esthetic aspects of the environment.

population density: The ratio of people to a land area.

population pyramid: A graphic expression of the age and sex distribution of a given population.

sex ratio: Ratio of the number of males in a population in any single year per 100 females.

suburbs: Smaller communities on the outskirts of central cities and somewhat dependent on them.

standard metropolitan statistical area (SMSA): Term used by the United States Bureau of the Census to designate units of population consisting of a county or counties that include a city of 50,000 or more people.

urbanism: A condition, a set of attitudes, a quality, or a way of life distinct from the rural.

urbanization: A population trend in which cities grow at the expense of rural areas.

zero population growth: A condition in which each person replaces himself or herself only (replacement level of 2.1); thus, the birthrate and the death rate are the same.

HOW MUCH DO YOU RECALL? TEST YOUR KNOWLEDGE
MULTIPLE CHOICE QUESTIONS:

1. Overpopulation is a problem worldwide but only in relation
   to:
   a. demography
   b. poor contraception
   c. population density
   d. political organization

2. Population began to increase steadily:
   a. by around the middle of the 17th century
   b. with improvements in agriculture, technology, and medicine
   c. in the Bronze Age
   d. both a and b

3. The number of births in a population in relation to every l000 women of childbearing age is called the:
    a. fecundity rate
    b. fertility rate
    c. population pyramid
    d. population growth rate

4. Which is typical of the first stage of the demographic transition?
    a. high birthrates and high death rates
    b. high birthrates and declining death rates
    c. declining birthrates and high death rates
    d. cycles of growth and decline

5. Which subject is not studied by demography?
    a. birthrates, death rates, sex rates
    b. age groups, marriage incidence, divorce frequency
    c. human mobility
    d. rock-forming, land-shaping, soil-forming

6. Zero population growth:
    a. means that no more children are born
    b. indicates that the fertility rate has dropped below the   replacement level
    c. must be achieved by all nations by the year 2000
    d. is actively pursued by the underdeveloped nations.

7. Demographers believe that:
    a. the demographic transition represents a general pattern
    b. Western societies are doomed to extinction
    c. the underdeveloped nations must increase their birthrate
    d. population grows in inverse proportion to food production

8. It is true of the population of the United States that:
    a. it is getting older
    b. there are more women than men
    c. rural and sunbelt areas attract the young
    d. only a and b

9. Birthrates:
    a. generally correspond to population density
    b. are low in western Europe and Japan
    c. are high in Arabia and Interior Africa
    d. only b and c

10. Most population experts:
    a. expect the growth rate to remain constant
    b. expect population to level off at between 8 and 15 billion people
    c. have written off the Malthusian prophecy altogether
    d. believe that a high fertility rate continues to be necessary in the developing nations

11. Urban families everywhere in the world:
    a. follow the dictates of religion and culture
    b. voluntarily curb their fertility
    c. have attained zero population growth
    d. willingly accept governmental family planning

12. Environmental pollution is the result of:
    a. dysfunctions in the earth's atmosphere
    b. ignorance on the part of the underdeveloped nations
    c. human actions that have harmful consequences
    d. unknown bacteria and viruses

13. The infant mortality rate in the United States:
    a. is the lowest in the world
    b. varies according to social class
    c. has no impact upon life expectancy
    d. is over 30

14. The United States became a bi-coastal society:
    a. when over 60 percent of the population lived on the east and west coasts
    b. because immigrants tend to settle near the port of entry
    c. because the rise of an information society sparked an internal migration to the coasts
    d. because federal policies have favored coastal states

15. In Third-World countries, the sex ratio reflects:
    a. higher birthrates for girls than boys
    b. female infanticide and general neglect of female children
    c. females' greater susceptibility to disease
    d. higher rates of conception for girls

16. One of the perceived advantages of suburban living is:
    a. concentration of apartments
    b. large variety of cultural resources
    c. older, more gracious housing
    d. greater safety from crime

17. Factors in the urban crisis include:
    a. the move of the middle class and industry to the suburbs
    b. the inner city's declining tax base
    c. a high percentage of deprived and trapped individuals
    d. all of the above

18. Urbanism is defined as:
    a. the migration of people from rural to urban centers
    b. a set of attitudes and a way of life distinct from the rural
    c. the growth of cities and suburbs at the expense of rural   areas
    d. the study of the growth and decline of populations

19. The urban crisis:
    a. is intensified by the move of the middle class to the suburbs
    b. has been reduced by urban renewal
    c. has been intensified by gentrification
    d. is well on the way to being resolved

20. Ghettos:
    a. have similar conditions and problems to slums
    b. are formed in part through residential segregation
    c. tend to contain a particular ethnic or racial group
    d. all of the above

21. A megalopolis is:
    a. a few small cities clustered around a central city
    b. two or more metropolitan areas joined without interruption
    c. a suburb which has become independent of the central city
    d. all of the above

22. Urban ecology concerns:
    a. the creation of green spaces in urban areas
    b. the location and patterned growth of urban areas
    c. rebuilding central cities
    d. elimination of urban pollution

23. The essence of the consumer culture is:
    a. suburbanization
    b. the class system
    c. the focus on the acquisition of material things
    d. early retirement

24. Subcultural theory:
    a. explains why community declines with urbanization
    b. argues that cities are mosaics of urban villages
    c. explains why cities promote feelings of alienation
    d. none of the above

ANSWERS TO FILL IN THE BLANKS:

A.   1. standard of living, Industrial Revolution
2. birthrates, death rates, sex ratios, age groups, marriage and divorce incidence, and human mobility
3. density
4. births, 1,000, year
5. high

B.   1. 35
2. arithmetic
3. Western, high
4. Zero population growth

C.   1. cultural, technical
2. size, age, sex
3. population pyramid
4. median age, three

D.   1. Urbanization
2. suburbanization
3. lower death rates, higher birthrates, immigration
4. 2500
5. condition, attitudes, way of life
6. rural, primary relationships, historical continuity, emotional involvement
7. suburbanization
8. SMSAs, megalopolis (urban sprawl)
9. slums, ghettos, opportunity
10. Gentrification, urban renewal

E.   1. natural conditions, resources
2. land forms, climate, vegetation, soils, animals, waters, and minerals
3. reciprocal, people
4. simple, direct
5. perceived, exploited
6. high population density
7. people

8. overpopulation, population density

F. 1. interact, interrelate
    2. balance, continue
    3. local, regional, global
    4. environmental pollution, environmental depletion, overpopulation
    5. tampering, damaging
    6. burning, fossil fuels
    7. air pollution
    8. water pollution
    9. resource depletion
    10. EPA, business community

ANSWERS TO MULTIPLE CHOICE QUESTIONS:

1. c
2. d
3. b
4. a
5. d
6. b
7. a
8. d
9. d
10. b
11. b
12. c
13. b
14. c
15. b
16. b
17. d
18. b
19. a
20. d
21. b
22. b
23. c

Chapter 12: Pivotal Institutions

Marriage and The Family

In this chapter, you will learn
1. about the important cultural functions that institutions perform;
2. of the importance of the family as the primary institution;
3. about the components of the family institution and its historical forms;
4. of the changes in the form of the American family;
5. about the problematic aspects of divorce;
6. of the effects of the changes in the American family

Topical Outline

I.   The Basic Institution: The Family
    A. Family Forms
    B. Kinship Systems
    C. Family Functions
        1. Regulation of Sex
        2. Reproduction
        3. Socialization
        4. Affection and Companionship

II.   Marriage
        1. Limitations on Marriage
        2. Love and Marriage in America
        3. The Stages Of Marriage
        4. The Role of Power in Marriage
        5. Changing Marital Patterns

III.   Divorce
        1. Remarriage
        2. Divorce As The New Norm
        3. Consequences Of Divorce: Wounds That Do Not Heal

IV.   The New American Family
        1. Forms Of The New American Family
        2. Living Together
        3. The Single-Parent Family
        4. The Small, Childless, or One-child Family
        5. Partnerships of Single People

V.   Some Unintended Effects of the Changing American Family
        1. Child Care
        2. Family Violence

3. Teenage Pregnancy

A. CHAPTER OUTLINE

The culture that each society produces becomes a **blueprint** for the behavior of each new generation. Among the most important elements of culture are **institutions**, which are the **habits,** or traditional ways of doing things, that eventually crystallize into **patterns of behavior.** Institutions **develop** around **human needs** that are essential to the individual. The most pivotal human institutions are the **family, religion**, **education, economy, and government**.

The **family** is the **oldest** of all societal institutions. Most of the **functions** of the family in modern industrial societies have been reduced to **control of sex** and **reproduction, socialization** of the young, and **provision of affection** and companionship.

The family has undergone **changes** in form as a result of **modernization**. It has become **nuclear** and more **egalitarian,** with the preferred form of marriage being **monogamy**. Although marriage partners are not chosen by parents, as they are in traditional societies, even in urban industrial societies **mate selection** is not **random**. It is influenced by **endogamy**, or **marriage within one's group**, and **homogamy**, or **marriage to partners with similar traits**. In most marriages, the partners are of the same race, religion, and social class, as well as similar in age and physical appearance, education and residence.

A. FILL IN THE BLANKS

1. _____are the most important elements of culture.
2. Traditional ways of doing things are another way of defining _____.
3. Institutions develop around _____ _____ that are essential to individuals.
4. Pivotal institutions include the _____, _____, _____, _____, and the _____.
5. Of all societal institutions, the _____is the oldest.
6. In contemporary societies, the functions of the family have been reduced to the control of ____and _____, the _____of the young, and the provision of _____and _____.
7. Among the changes brought by modernization, the family has become more _____ and _____ in form.
8. The preferred form of marriage in the nuclear family is _____.
9. Mate selection is influenced by _____ and _____.
10. Marriage within one's group is called _____, and marriage to partners with similar traits is called _____.

B. Chapter Outline

The **nuclear form of family** is better adapted to life in an **urban industrial** society than is the extended family because it allows members more freedom to pursue upward social mobility. Its isolation from the support system of an extended family and the intensity of the emotions within it, however, make it particularly **susceptible to conflict**. Divorce and **desertion** are two prominent results of conflict, as are child abuse and mate **abuse**. Divorce is also a corollary of liberalized **sexual norms** and of changing attitudes toward marriage. As the necessity for having many children declines, the **focus of marriage** shifts away from the idea that it is the **duty** of everyone to marry to replenish society. Increasingly, marriage is entered into for **affection** and **companionship.**

B. FILL IN THE BLANKS

1. The nuclear form of the family is _____ _____ to life in modern societies.
2. It allows its member to attain upward _____ _____.
3. The price one pays for more freedom is the individual's _____ from an extended family group.
4. In addition, the intensity of emotions within the nuclear family make it susceptible to _____.
5. Among the most serious results of family conflict are _____ and _____.
6. Family conflict also results in _____ against mates and children.
7. Divorce is also an effect of liberalized _____ _____ and changing _____ toward marriage.
8. The focus of marriage turns away from the necessity of _____ society.
9. In modern societies, marriage is entered into for purposes of _____ and _____.

C. CHAPTER OVERVIEW

Interracial marriages are **infrequent** not so much because of prejudice and discrimination--although these factors are of course present--but because **endogamy** and **homogamy** are so strongly embedded in our institutional framework. **New forms** of the family keep appearing. For example, some homosexual couples choose to live in a marital union which sometimes includes children, biological (of one of the partners) or adopted. A number of state legislatures have introduced legislation to make such unions as legal as heterosexual marriages, but this notion still elicits much controversy.

Among **alternatives** to traditional family life, one finds the **single-parent family**, the **blended or reconstituted** family, **the small, childless, or one-child family**, and, increasingly, the **multiple-generations family**. The **problematic issues** deriving from the changes in the family include **difficulties in adjustment** for **children of divorced parents**, an increase in **family violence**, including child and spouse abuse, the **inadequacy of child care** for families in which both spouses must work, and the high incidence of **out-of-wedlock**, especially teenage, **pregnancies**. But changes and transformations only testify that the family institution endures.

C. FILL IN THE BLANKS

1. In our society, interracial marriages are still _____.
2. People do not tend to intermarry because _____ and _____ are so entrenched in our family institution.
3. New family forms that keep appearing include _____marital unions.
4. Such unions still provoke much _____.
5. Other alternatives to the traditional family form include: the _____ _____ family, the _____ or _____family, the _____.
6. The changes in the family have caused a number of _____ issues.
7. Among the difficulties in contemporary families are: adjustment for ____ __ _____, an increase in _____, inadequate ____ _____, and a high incidence of _____ pregnancies.

Terms to Remember

consanguine Another term for the extended family. Also, the way parents are related to their children, that is, by blood ties.

extended family A form of the family consisting of the nucleus--two spouses and their children--and other blood relatives together with their marriage partners and children. Common in preindustrial societies.

incest taboo An almost universal prohibition of sexual relations between mother and son, father and daughter, sister and brother, and other relatives as specified by the society.

institution A pattern of behavior (culture complex) that has developed around a central human need. A blueprint for living in society.

monogamy The most common form of marriage, consisting of the union of one man with one woman.

nuclear or conjugal family A form of the family consisting of two spouses and their children living together as a unit.
polygamy A form of marriage in which multiple spouses--either wives or husbands--cohabit as units.

HOW MUCH DO YOU REMEMBER? TEST YOUR KNOWLEDGE
MULTIPLE CHOICE QUESTIONS

1.   The family institution:
     a. began the cycle of institution building
     b. appears only in Western societies
     c. loses all importance in industrial societies
     d. is about to disappear

2.   A fundamental need that we attempt to fill within the family is the need for:
     a. discipline
     b. social control
     c. affection and companionship
     d. learning the meaning of life

3.   Institutions are best described as:
     a. patterns of behavior followed in societies
     b. tangible objects
     c. housing for felons
     d. mental hospitals

4.   Polygyny is the most common form of:
     a. polygamy
     b. monogamy
     c. group marriage
     d. polyandry

5.   The practice of encouraging marriage outside certain groups is called:
     a. polygyny
     b. exogamy
     c. oncology
     d. endogamy

6.   The practice of encouraging marriage within specific groups is called:
     a. monogamy
     b. bigamy
     c. dichotomy
     d. endogamy

7.   In preindustrial societies, marriage was:
     a. based on love and mutual admiration

b. an economic arrangement between families
c. the result of romantic feelings
d. preceded by pregnancy

8. The tendency to marry someone very much like oneself is called:
   a. heterogamy
   b. homogamy
   c. exogamy
   d. endogamy

9. Historically, the family has existed in which of these two forms?
   a. Extended, also called consanguine
   b. Conjugal, also called nuclear
   c. Balanced, also called bipolar
   d. Only a and b
   e. A, b, and c

10. In the last several decades, divorce has increased most rapidly among the:
    a. elderly
    b. middle aged
    c. young and recently married
    d. d. young and recently remarried

11. A much better adjustment to divorce Is made by couples who:
    a. have more than one child
    b. married for love
    c. hate each other
    d. are childless

12. Couples who lived together before marrying are:
    a. less likely to get divorced than couples who did not cohabit
    b. decreasing in number
    c. are more willing to accept divorce as the solution to marital problems
    d. are considered deviant by the middle class

13. A critical time in a marriage is:
    a. when a couple become parents
    b. when the wife decides to work outside the home
    c. when the couple engage in extramarital affairs
    d. when children leave home

14. The two issues about which most couples argue most commonly are:
    a. frequency of sex and household chores
    b. children and money

c. religion and in-laws
d. politics and sports

15. The most amount of marital satisfaction is exhibited by:
    a. the newly married
    b. those in their middle years
    c. those who married for love
    d. those who married for money

16. According to the resources theory:
    a. children are valued because of their economic contribution to the family
    b. the balance of marital power depends on resources each partner brings to the marriage
    c. successful children draw upon family resources
    d. love and concern for others are the most important family resources

17. Which is not one of the changes that has occurred in the family institution in this century?
    a. Women have entered the work force in droves.
    b. Divorce has dramatically increased.
    c. Egalitarianism has been totally achieved.
    d. Voluntary childlessness has increased.

ANSWERS TO FILL IN THE BLANKS

A. 1. Institutions
   2. institutions
   3. human needs
   4. family, religion, education, government, and economy
   5. family
   6. sex and reproduction, socialization, affection and companionship
   7. egalitarian, nuclear
   8. monogamy
   9. endogamy and homogamy
   10. endogamy, homogamy

B. 1. Better adapted
   2. social mobility
   3. isolation
   4. conflicts
   5. divorce, desertion
   6. violence (abuse)
   7. sexual norms, attitudes
   8. replenishing society

9. affection, companionship

C. 1. Rare
   2. endogamy
   3. homosexual
   4. controversy
   5. single-parent, childless or one-child, blended or reconstituted, multiple generations
   6. problematic
   7. children of divorce, violence, child care, teenage

ANSWERS TO MULTIPLE CHOICE QUESTIONS

1. a
2. c
3. a
4. a
5. b
6. d
7. b
8. b
9. d
10. c
11. d
12. c
13. a
14. b
15. b
16. b
17. c

Chapter 13: Pivotal Institutions

Religion And Education

In this chapter, you will learn

1. the reasons for the emergence of the institution of religion;
2. how religion is viewed from the perspective of the social sciences;
3. the functions of religion in society;
4. the characteristics of religion America;
5. the trends in contemporary religion;
6. the ultimate place of religion in contemporary societies;
7. the definition and characteristics of education;
8. about the role of education relative to social class, race, and ethnicity;
9. the nature of the crisis of American education;
10. about the status of higher education.

TOPICAL OUTLINE

I.   The Great Religions of the World

II.   Religion In The Social Sciences
      1. Religion as Social Integration
      2. A Functionalist View of Religion
      3. A Conflict View of Religion

III.   Religion and Social Control
      1. Protestant Ethic and the Spirit of Capitalism

IV.   The Institutional Context
      1. Common Features of Religions

V.   Religion in America
      1. Religiosity in America
      2. Religious Affiliation and Social Class

VI.   The Sanctification of the American Way of Life
      1. Contemporary Trends
      2. Fundamentalism
      3. The Electronic Church
      4. The Role of Women in Religion

V. Education
      1. Education In America
      2. The Functionalist View of Education

147

A. CHAPTER OVERVIEW

Religion has been found in **every society** because, as thinking animals, humans are curious about the **meaning and purpose** of life. However, sociologists study religion only as a **manifestation of culture** and to uncover relationships, effects, and behavior.

The major religions of the world may be categorized into **monotheistic, polytheistic, ethical, and ancestral**. The **monotheistic** religions include **Christianity,** with the largest membership, followed by **Islam and Judaism**. **Hinduism** is the largest **polytheistic** religion; Buddhism, Confucianism, and **Taoism** are the **ethical** religions. **Shintoism** practiced by the Japanese is an **ancestral** religion.

A. FILL IN THE BLANKS

1. Religion is a universal institution because people need to know about the_____ and _____ of life.
2. Unlike theologians, sociologists study religion as a _____of culture.
3. Sociologists also study religion to uncover _____, _____, and _____.
4. The main categories of religion are _____, _____, _____ and _____.
5. The religion with the largest membership among the monotheistic religions is _____.
6. The other monotheistic religions are _____ and _____.
7. The largest polytheistic religion is _____.
8. Among the ethical religions, we find _____, _____, _____.
9. The Japanese practice _____, which is an _____religion.

B. CHAPTER OVERVIEW

Religion, when first studied by the social scientists, was considered to be the result of people's attempts to **explain a reality** they **did not understand**. It was suggested that religion dealt with the sacred and that the object of religious beliefs and practices was society itself. This **viewpoin**t has been incorporated into **functionalism,** whose theorists assume that the functions of religion include relief of feelings of frustration, the explanation of the physical world, the support of norms and values of society, provision of a means for repentance, and help during the difficult stages of life.

The ideas of **Karl Marx** are forerunners of the **conflict position** in regard to religion. Marx believed that religion and the idea of God were **human creations,** but that people forgot they invented God and began to fear him. Fear produced **alienation**, and Marx considered religion as the most alienating of institutions, especially because it **allowed the dominant classes** in society to **exploit** the masses and keep them in subordinate positions by defending the status quo. But Marx was not entirely correct: **religion also functions** to promote **social change**, often to the benefit of the downtrodden. Religion also functions as a creator of meaning and thus it is a reflection of each culture. The famous study **The Protestant Ethic and the Spirit of Capitalism** traces the rise of capitalism as an **effect** of the religious ideas of **Protestantism**, especially of Calvinism. Religious ideas contributed to **change** in the society in addition to **enforcing** the **norms** of society, **legitimizing** the **political power of leaders** and the behavioral demands of institutions.

B. FILL IN THE BLANKS

1. Social scientists at first believed that religion was an _____ by people to _____ a reality they did not understand.
2. Scientists also believed that the object of religion was _____ itself.
3. Religion deals with the _____ as opposed to the everyday, or _____.
4. Functionalist theory assumes that religion functions to relieve _____, explain _____ phenomena, support the _____ and _____ of society, provide a means for _____ and help during _____ _____ of life.
5. The conflict theory owes much to the ideas of _____ _____.
6. _____ believed that religion and the idea of God were _____ creations.
7. He believed, additionally, that people had _____ their invention and began to fear it.
8. Fear produces _____, and religion, in this view, is the most _____ of institutions.
9. In this thinker's view, religion supports the _____ _____, allowing the dominant social classes to exploit the _____.
10. Religion, however, also is an instrument of _____ that often is to the advantage of the downtrodden.
11. Religion also reflects _____, creates _____, and has important _____.
12. A famous study determined that capitalism was principally the result of _____, especially _____.

149

13. Religious ideas, then, _____ to change, enforced _____ _____,
    legitimized the _____ _____ of leaders and the behavioral demands of
    other institutions.

C. CHAPTER OVERVIEW

Religions continue to have **functions** in society. One of these functions is to
provide an identity and a feeling of community to people through membership
in religious groups. However, we have also developed a kind of **"civil religion"**
by making holy some of our **political ideals, national heroes, and our
common destiny.**

All religions **display beliefs, rituals, and organization**. Religious organizations
are divided into **church, sect, and cult**. Religion in America is **denominational,**
and the methods of the marketplace are used to recruit and hold members.

Modern **trends** in religion include **secularization** and **bureaucratization**.
Religious organizations resemble other kinds of voluntary associations that deal
with mental health, family togetherness, and social welfare. A **reaction** to this
lack of spirituality may be seen in the emergence of a number of **sectarian**
movements of **a pentecostal and evangelical** nature.

C. FILL IN THE BLANKS

1. The functions of religion in the present include providing an _____and a
    feeling of _____to people through membership.
2. A kind of _____religion has also developed in the United States.
3. This kind of religion worships some of our _____ _____, _____ _____ and
    our _____ _____.
4. All religions include _____, _____ and _____.
5. Religious organizations are divided into _____, _____, and _____.
6. Religion in America is _____.
7. Members are recruited by the same methods as those used in the

    _____.
8. Recent trends in religion include _____and _____.
9. Religious organizations are just like other _____ _____.
10. They deal with _____ _____, family _____, and _____
    welfare.
11. As a result of this lack of spirituality, we have seen the growth of _____
    and _____movements.

D. CHAPTER OVERVIEW

The **transmission of knowledge** from one generation to the next is the primary
function of **education.** Education also functions to **recruit and prepare** students

for the **social and occupational roles** in the outside world, to integrate into the wider culture the various subcultures that are part of it, and finally to **generate new knowledge** through research. Schools also perform **custodial** functions, contribute to the formation of a youth subculture, and sometimes effectively change attitudes.

The best **predictor** of academic **success** is **socioeconomic status**, which is a function of the family. This is not a direct economic relationship, but rather takes into account differences in family life-styles, in styles of communication, in values and expectations of parents, and so on. **Middle-class families** prepare their children for a **successful experience** in school, where they are **taught** by middle-class teachers with **similar cultural goals** and expectations. Life in the **lower-class family** does not adequately prepare a child for a successful school experience, and since a large number of minorities are still positioned in the lower and working classes, they have been generally the least successful in academic pursuits (exceptions are the new immigrants, prevailingly Asian, who value education as an avenue for upward mobility and who have high rates of success in academia).

Although **education** has been considered the gateway to **upward mobility**--and for many people it has been--the increase in the number of high school and college graduates has begun to **change** this relationship. Many other factors seem to be responsible for the kinds of jobs people get. Thus, a **rethinking** of what our **educational goals** is in order.

D. FILL IN THE BLANKS

1. The transmission of culture from one generation to the other is done principally by the institution of _____.
2. Education functions to _____ and _____ individuals for their future roles in society.
3. Additional functions of education are: to _____ subcultural groups into the mainstream society, and to _____ new knowledge through _____.
4. Some unintended functions of education are _____, while others include forming a _____ subculture and changing _____.
5. Socioeconomic status is the best _____ of academic _____.
6. Status derives from a student's _____.
7. Middle-class families seem to have the _____, lifestyles, and ways of _____ that encourage academic success.
8. Parental expectations in middle-class families are _____.
9. Teachers are also generally _____ _____ and so they reinforce parental expectations.
10. Life in lower-class families does not _____ children for academic _____.
11. A number of minorities are economically lower-class, which explains the high rates of _____ their students.

12. More recent immigrants who value education as a means of _____ _____ are much more academically successful.
13. The large number of students who graduate from high school and college has changed the _____ of education as a way of improving people's chances at _____ mobility.

E. Chapter Overview

Higher education is also in **disarray** nowadays. First of all, the **goal** of higher **education** is much changed--rather than leading to a well-rounded personality, it now leads to a **narrow specialization** and professionalization. Universities experienced a boom after World War II and again in the 1960s as a result of the GI Bill and demographic factors. Now, however, **enrollments are down**, and few Americans are receiving postgraduate degrees, particularly in the hard sciences. Moreover, many campuses are seats of controversy as the establishment of a **new curriculum** pits **traditionalists** against **multiculturalists:** minorities, women and homosexuals. Finally, ethnic and racial groups are increasingly segregating themselves, a reflection of the fragmentation of the wider society.

A variety of **reforms** have been tried in the past three decades in an effort to improve American education. Unfortunately, to date **nothing** seems to have **worked**, possibly because of the **anti-intellectual** values prevalent in the society and the apathy of parents, products of the same educational system.

E. FILL IN THE BLANKS

1. Higher education is also in _____.
2. The purpose of higher education has changed from creating a _____ personality, to preparing the individual for a narrow _____ or profession.
3. This change occurred when universities experienced a _____, following World War II and again in the _____.
4. Now that unemployment is low, university _____ are also _____.
5. Few college students are receiving _____ degrees, especially in the ____ sciences.
6. Many campuses are embroiled in _____ that pits _____ versus multiculturalists.
7. There is also a tendency for racial and ethnic minorities to _____, a reflection of the _____ of the wider society.
8. Of the reforms that have been attempted, _____ proved able to _____ American education.
9. Possibly, American education suffers because of the _____ that runs through the society.

TERMS TO REMEMBER

animism: Belief that many objects in the world are inhabited by spirits.

church: A religious organization that is institutionalized and well integrated into the socioeconomic life of a society, and in which participation is routine.

cult: The least conventional and least institutionalized of religious organizations. It consists of groups of followers clustered around a leader whose teachings differ substantially from the doctrines of the church or denomination.

denomination: A subdivision of the church that is considered equally as valid as the church.

dissemination, innovation, and preservation: The functions of education that instigate social change at the same time that they conserve the traditional cultural heritage.

ecclesia: A church to which a substantial majority of the population belongs.

education: The formal aspect of socialization in which a specific body of knowledge and skills is deliberately transmitted by specialists.

ethical religions: Those that stress the need to live an ethical life so as to attain harmony in personal life and in society (Buddhism, Confucianism, Taoism).

latent functions: Those functions that are the unintended consequences of the process of education.

mana: A concept according to which there exists a supernatural force that can attach to any person, object, or event.

manifest functions: The desired, expected, and agreed-upon functions of education.

monotheism: Belief in the existence of one God (Judaism, Christianity, Islam).

multiversity: a large university, consisting of a number of campuses dispersed around a state.

polytheism: Belief in the existence of many gods (Hinduism).

profane: The objects and events of everyday life that are common, usual, explainable, and repetitive.

rites of passage: Rituals established around critical times of growth and maturation: birth, puberty, marriage, and death.

ritual: Behavior that follows the creation of sacredness and provides a mechanism for maintaining the sacred.

sacred: Objects, events, or persons distinct from the profane, that is, that are uncommon, unusual, unexplained, mysterious, powerful, and therefore deserving of reverence and respect. Religion deals with the sacred.

sect: A religious organization that is a revolutionary movement breaking away from the church or denomination. It stresses the spirit, rather than the letter, of religion.

self-fulfilling prophecy: The research-supported idea that if teachers treat students as if they felt they were bright and capable, students will perform up to the teachers' expectations, and vice versa.

tracking: The grouping of students according to ability.

HOW MUCH DO YOU RECALL? TEST YOUR KNOWLEDGE.

MULTIPLE CHOICE QUESTIONS

1. Religion is found in every society because the divinity revealed itself to all people
   a. it helps people attain immortality
   b. religion represents a response to an urgent human need
   c. people could not survive without the aid of a superior force

2. Totemism is a form of:
   a. polytheism
   b. monotheism
   c. animism
   d. ethical religion

3. The major clasification of religious organizations is into:
   a. church, synagogue, temple
   b. church, denomination, and ecclesia
   c. church, sect, and cult

d. Catholicism, Protestantism, Judaism

4. A religious movement that is usually temporary and is centered around a charismatic leader whose teachings differ from established doctrines is called a(n):
     a. sect
     b. cult
     c. ecclesia
     d. denomination

5. A polytheistic religion followed by a large number of believers is:
     a. animism
     b. Shintoism
     c. Buddhism
     d. Hinduism

6. Among the major religions of the world, the one with most adherents is:
     a. Islam
     b. Zoroastrianism
     c. Judaism
     d. Christianity

7. The worship of one's ancestors is part of which of the following religions?
     a. Judaism
     b. Shintoism
     c. Taoism
     d. Islam

8. The sacred differs from the profane in that:
     a. it is commonplace
     b. the profane relies on a belief in evil forces
     c. it is separate from everyday experience, mysterious, and powerful
     d. it is inherent in objects and events of everyday life

9. In the United States, there is no church or religion legally recognized as "official" because:
     a. the U. S. Constitution provides for separation of church and state
     b. popular consensus is against it
     c. Americans fought a war for religious freedom
     d. The Declaration of Independence included this provision

10. According to the functionalist view of religion, religion helps people adjust to the following human conditions:

a. happiness, satiety, plenty
b. contingency, powerlessness, scarcity
c. status, privilege, power
d. peace, rivalry, territorial imperative

11. Karl Marx viewed religion as:
a. a human creation
b. an ideology that masks class interests
c. an alienating experience
d. all of the above
e. none of the above

12. Funerals, confirmations, Bar Mitzvahs, weddings, and other such rituals are called:
a. celebrations
b. rites of passage
c. divine interventions
d. festivities

13. Which is false of the American educational institution?
a. It is reserved for a small elite of intellectually superior students.
b. It is an open and universal system for the first 12 years.
c. Its goal is to provide and equal educational opportunity to all.
d. It is compulsory until the age of 16.

14. In countries other than the U.S., education is funded by:
a. local districts
b. urban communities
c. wealthy taxpayers
d. none of the above

15. One of the latent functions of schools is that they:
a. maintain the class system of society
b. encourage social mobility
c. promote nationalism
d. none of the above

16. One of the most important manifest functions of education is:
a. it supplements the process of socialization begun by the family
b. it prepares students for occupational roles
c. it reinforces the values and norms of the society
d. all of the above
e. none of the above

17, The idea that education is used by the elite to manipulate the masses and retain its high status in society is part of:

    a. functionalist theory
    b. conflict theory
    c. interactive theory
    d. pedagogical theory

18. In general, American parents prefer that their children receive an education that:

    a. makes them sensitive to the world around them
    b. makes them receptive to the arts
    c. makes them civic-minded citizens
    d. prepares them for occupational roles

19. The two minority groups that have taken the most advantage of educational opportunities to achieve a higher social status are:

    a. Hispanics and African-Americans
    b. Native Americans and Wasps
    c. Jews and Asians
    d. Russians and women

20. The most important determinant of scholastic success is:

    a. inborn intelligence
    b. a Jewish mother
    c. the family
    d. the peer group

ANSWERS TO FILL IN THE BLANKS

A.   1. Meaning, purpose
        2. manifestation
        3. relationships, effects, behavior
        4. monotheistic, polytheistic, ethical, ancestral
        5. Christianity
        6. Judaism, Islam
        7. Hinduism
        8. Buddhism, Confucianism, Taoism
        9. Shintoism ancestral

B.   1. Attempt, explain

        2. society
        3. sacred, profane
        4. frustration, physical, values, norms, repentance, difficult stages

5. Karl Marx
6. Marx, human
7. Forgotten
8. alienating, alienating
9. Status quo, masses
10. change
11. culture, meaning, effects
12. Protestantism, Calvinism
13. change, social norms, political power

C.   1. identity, community
      2. civil
      3. political ideals, national heroes, common destiny
      4. rituals, beliefs, organization
      5. church, sect, cult
      6. denominational
      7. marketplace
      8. secularization, bureaucratization
      9. voluntary organizations
      10. mental health, togetherness, social
      11. pentecostal, evangelical

D.   1. education
      2. recruit and prepare
      3. integrate, generate, research
      4. custodial, youth, attitudes
      5. predictor, success
      6. family
      7. valves, communication
      8. high
      9. middle class
      10. prepare, success
      11. failure
      12. upward mobility
      13. function, upward

E.   1. disarray
      2. well-rounded, occupation
      3. boom, 1960s
      4. enrollments, low
      5. graduate, hard
      6. controversy, traditionalists
      7. self-segregate, fragmentation
      8. none, improve

9.anti-intellectualism

ANSWERS TO MULTIPLE CHOICE QUESTIONS

1. c
2. a
3. c
4. b
5. d
6. d
7. b
8. c
9. a
10. b
11. d
12. b
13. a
14. d
15. a
16. d
17. b
18. c
19. c
20. c

CHAPTER 14: GOVERNMENT

THE INSTITUTION, AND THE THEORIES AND IDEOLOGIES THAT UNDERLIE IT

In this chapter, you will learn

1. the reason for the emergence of the institution of government;

2. the purpose and functions of government;

3. the importance of legitimacy and authority in the exercise of political power, as well as the types of authority;

4. the differences between the state and government;

5. the definition of a nation-state;

6. that the underpinnings of social movements, governments, and economic behavior consist of ideologies;

7. the differences between autocratic and democratic ideologies;

8. about the dominant totalitarian ideology of the right and the social movement it spawned;

9. about the dominant totalitarian ideology of the left and the social movements that followed;

10. the principles of the democratic ideology and of its subideologies of capitalism and democratic socialism.

TOPICAL OUTLINE

I.   The Institution of Government
        A. Government and Politics
        B. The Purpose of Government
        C. The Functions of Government

II.   Political Power: Legitimacy And Authority
        A. Legitimacy
        B. Authority
                1. Types of Legitimate Authority
                        a. Traditional Authority
                        b. Legal-Rational Authority
                        c. Charismatic Authority

III.   The State
        A. Theoretical Views of the State
        B. The Nation-State
        B. Nationalism

IV.   The Ideologies Behind the State
        A. The Role Of Ideology
        B. Political Ideology
                1. Autocratic Ideologies
                2. Authoritarianism and Totalitarianism

a. Totalitarianism Of The Right: Fascism And Nazism
b. Totalitarianism of The Left: Communism
c. Historical Prediction: the Dialectic
3. Democracy
a. Democratic Capitalism
b. Socialism
c. Democratic Socialism

A. CHAPTER OVERVIEW

The institution of government arises out of humanity's need for **social order**. When social control can no longer be administered within the family because of the **size and complexity** of a society, some kind of body with the authority to make decisions binding on the society becomes essential. Social order is a byproduct of **group life** and is implemented through various means of **social control.** Social control is the process by which the group, society or smaller groups within it, induces the individual to behave in a designated way. To exert social control, it is necessary to possess **power.** Social control that is **institutionalized** is called **government.**

In simple societies, social order may be maintained through **moral control.** In a complex society, this internalized cultural learning acquired through socialization, must be supplemented by **political control** exerted by forces outside the individual. People invest a person or entity with the authority to exercise political control. Various processes of government determine when and how and by whom political control is to be exercised. The most important function of government, then, is to **implement social control.** In addition, government **protects** citizens from external threats, **plans and maintains** physical facilities of the infrastructure, **regulates** the economy, etc.

A. FILL IN THE BLANKS:

1. Government is an institution that arises out of the need for_____ _____.
2. Social order is a result of _____life and is implemented by exerting _____
   _____.
3. To exert social control, one needs to have _____.
4. The process by which a group induces an individual to behave in a certain way is called_____ _____.
5. Government may be defined as social control that is _____.
6. Government legitimizes the acquisition and exercise of _____.
7. In simple societies, social order may be maintained through _____ _____alone.
8. In complex societies, social order must be supplemented by_____ _____.
9. Various processes of government determine _____, and by _____political control is to be exercised.
10. In addition to implementing social control, government also _____citizens from external threats, _____facilities, _____the economy, etc.

B. CHAPTER OVERVIEW

To be acceptable to members of society, government must have **authority**. Authority may have a basis in **tradition**, in **reason** and the law, or in the **charisma** of a leader. Authority may be defined as **legitimate power**. Power is the ability of one person or group to influence the behavior of another person or group in a desired direction. **Force** or the **threat** of force underlies power.

Power is **central** to the political process because in order to exert social control, it is necessary to have the power to do so. One **definition** of power is that one party in a social relationship will **carry out his/her own** will **despite resistance**. Power is important in a variety of social interactions, and it can be asserted in a number of ways--through **rewards, coercion, or influence**.

Political power is power exercised by the **state** through its government. The **state** is the **abstract** representation of the political system of a society. The state has the **authority** to employ **force** to **implement social control**, and its authority is legitimate. That is, when the members of a society accept the use of power on the part of an individual or entity as right and proper, that power is considered **legitimate**. When power is used illegally and **illegitimately**, it is termed **coercion**. When it is used legally and legitimately, it is called **authority**.

Authority, then, refers to power over, or **control of**, individuals that is socially accepted as **right and proper**. As noted above, authority derives from a number of sources summarized by the social thinker Max Weber as: **traditional**, in which legitimization derives from the past and authority is accepted because it has always been so; **legal-rational**, in which authority is established on rules arrived at in a rational manner and is based on the rule of law; and **charismatic**, or embodied in the person of an exceptional leader.

B. FILL IN THE BLANKS

1. An element central to the political process is _____.
2. One definition of power is the ability of one party in a relationship to carry out his/her will _ _____ __ _____.
3. **Power** can be asserted through _____, _____,   and _____.
4. Political power is exercised by the _____through its ____.
5. The state has the _____to implement social control because it has a monopoly on force.
6. The state's authority is _____.
7. Legitimate power is power that members of a society accept as being _____and _____.
8. Legitimate power is called _____.
9. Illegitimate and illegal power is
10. The sources of authority may be summarized as being _____,_____, and _____.

C. CHAPTER OVERVIEW

The state is the formal abstract **structure representing** government. **Its elements are** territory, population, government, **and** sovereignty. The state's **chief aim** is to impose **organized** political control over its citizens, and it can do so because it has a **monopoly** over the legitimate use of **force** within its territory.

Contemporary views on the state include **functionalism** and the **conflict theory.** Functionalists are the theoretical descendants of **Hobbes** who perceive the **state** as a **functional institution** necessary for **maintaining law and order**, providing the ultimate source of arbitration, an orderly allocation of resources, economic coordination, and acting as a vehicle for interaction with other states. Conflict theorists look to the French philosopher **Jean-Jacques Rousseau**, who also disagreed with Hobbes, in their belief that before the emergence of the state--which occurred to protect the position of the privileged--people lived as "**noble savages**" who only began to fight when the notion of private property developed. Karl Marx agreed with Rousseau, believing that all but the most primitive societies consisted of at least **two classes** of which one dominated and exploited the other through social institutions. The state, in Marx's view, was an instrument in the service of the **ruling class**.

C.FILL IN THE BLANKS:

1. Government is the _____that includes the _____who exercise political power.
2. The state is the _____embodiment, the _____ _____, of the institution of government.
3. The state is _____, the government _____.
4. The basic components of the state are _____, _____, and _____.

5. Two opposing views on the relationship of government to the governed are presented by _____ and _____.

6. The author of **The Leviathan** speculated that people accepted _____ _____ because life in the _____ ____ ____ was "nasty, brutish, solitary, and short."

7. In the contract, people relinquished some liberty in exchange for _____ and_____ _____.

8. The author of **Two Treatises of Government** maintained that life in the state of nature was guided by _____ and people entered into the _____-___contract because it was the_____ thing to do.

9. Some of the ideas of the above author reflected in the American Constitution are:_____ government, government resting on the_____ of the governed, and offering_____ of property.

10. Contemporary views of the origin of the state include _____ and _____ theory.

D. CHAPTER OVERVIEW

The organization of societies into nation-states is a comparatively recent event in history. A central government that oversees a particular territory in which people have similar characteristics develops a sense of unity and nationhood. Nationalism is the ideology behind the nation-state; it may be defined as a set of beliefs about the superiority of one's own nation and a defense of its interests above all others.

Much of our **social world** is based on **ideas, concepts, and symbols** that explain and justify the way things are, as well as the way things ought to be. When such ideas are systematic, rational, intelligible, and organized into a logical pattern of thought, they are said to be **ideologies**. More completely, an ideology is a **value or belief system** that is **accepted as fact** or truth by some group. It consists of **sets of attitudes** toward the institutions and processes of society and provides the believer with a **picture of the world** as it is and as it should be, thus making a complex world easily understandable.

Our lives are guided by a number of ideologies. However, political and economic ideologies have special functions, characteristics, and consequences. They tend to **arise** during periods of **crisis** and among those to whom the dominant world view has become unacceptable. Some are very **comprehensive** (totalitarian), others are **partial**. They are **abstract**, being a model derived from one person's perception of reality. They are **reductionist**, in that they reduce what is complex into an understandable form. And they are **meaningless outside** of **social movements**.

The **functions** of ideologies include: making the governors acceptable to the governed (**lending government** a **justification** without which it could not function); providing a **cognitive structure**, a system through which the world is perceived, understood, and interpreted, thus helping people avoid insecurity and strain; **guiding specific behaviors** and attitudes of individuals and groups; and serving as a **vital force** in life, offering a sense of mission and purpose, and a commitment to action.

Political ideology refers to concepts dealing with questions as to **who** will be the rulers, **how** they will be selected, and by **what** principles they will govern. It is meant to **persuade** and **counter** opposing views, and to affect some major value. It has a **program** for the retention, reform, or abolition of social institutions. It partially rationalizes group interest. It is **normative, ethical, and moral** in tone and content. And it is a part of a broader belief system whose properties it shares.

Ideologies are **not monolithic**, but contain differences within them; people are **socialized** into the **dominant** political ideology of their society, and tend to act accordingly; and most people hold **conflicting** ideologies at the same time.

D. FILL IN THE BLANKS:

1. Ideologies are _____ of ideas that are _____ ,_____ , and _____ .

2. Ideologies consist of ____ ___ _____ toward societal institutions and processes.

3. Ideologies provide the believer with a _____ of the world as it is and as it_____ _____ .

4. Political and economic ideologies tend to arise during_____ of _____ and among those to whom the _____ ideology has become _____ .

5. Ideologies are also described as being _____ or partial, _____- _____ , and _____ .

6. The functions of ideologies include: lending _____ , providing a cognitive _____ , offering a sense of _____ ___ _____ to life.

7. The most important concept in political ideology deals with the questions of: _____ , how will the governors be _____ and by what _____ they will govern.

8. Political ideology is meant to _____ and counter _____ views.

9. Political ideology offers a program for either _____ , _____ , or _____ some major institution.

10. There are differences within ideologies; thus they are not _____ . In addition, people tend to act according to the ideology into which they were _____ . Finally, most people hold _____ ideologies simultaneously.

E. CHAPTER OVERVIEW

Autocracy is an ideology based on the belief that **government** should be **in the hands of one individual or group** who has **supreme power** over the people of a society. Through history, autocracy has had many forms; but in modern times, traditional autocracy has been replaced by ideologies of the right and of the left that we call **totalitarian**. These ideologies are based on modern technology and mass legitimation. They came into existence when what were thought to be short-lived dictatorships became permanent regimes. Some **common features** of totalitarian regimes include: the official ideology expresses a **revolt** against present society, and **idealistic hopes** for a future, more perfect society; the ideology is **totalist**: it attempts to reform the total individual and prescribes a life-style with implications in all spheres of life. Totalitarian regimes maintain a **single** party functioning as the organization through which the ideology is kept alive; the head of the party is a **leader (dictator)** or an **oligarchy** (small elite) who interprets the ideology to the masses. The state has a **secret police**; controls the **mass media**; controls all **arms**; centrally plans and controls the **economy**.

Fascism and Nazism are two totalitarian ideologies of the **right**. Fascism came to power in Italy in 1922, and Nazism emerged in Germany a decade later. Most of the differences between the two ideologies are due to the different **personalities** of the two leaders, Benito Mussolini in Italy and Adolf Hitler in Germany.

The principal elements of the fascist outlook include: a **distrust** of **reason**, the **denial** of basic **human equality**, a code of behavior based on **violence** and distortion of truth, government by the **elite**, totalitarianism, racism, imperialism, and opposition to international law and order. Fascist principles of organization and control are applied to the economy of fascist regimes. The economy is divided into state-controlled associations of capital and labor, and the ultimate mediator is the one-party state. The most virulent forms of fascism were eliminated with the defeat of the Axis powers inWorld War II. However, fascistic tendencies can be observed in a number of nations today.

Communism is a totalitarian ideology of the **left**. It is based on very old ideals of egalitarianism, but its modern expression is to be found in the conditions following the Industrial Revolution. The principal author of communist ideology was Karl Marx who speculated that people's conditions and beliefs were determined by **economic relationships**; that in fact all relationships in life rested on an economic base. In addition, change was constant in societies, and it proceeded through a number of struggles. In societies that were at the capitalist stage of economic development, the struggle was between the **bourgeoisie** (owners of the means of production) and the **proletariat** (industrial workers). Marx tried to predict historical outcomes through a tool of analysis called the **dialectic**, a method of questions and answers in which a position is stated, criticized until the opposite position is taken, and finally a middle position between the two opposites is attained. But Marx was **wrong** in predicting the **demise of capitalism** and the victory of the proletariat: none of the societies that had adopted Marxism ha ever achieved that **ultimate goal**--a **classless** society.

166

E. FILL IN THE BLANKS:

1. Autocracy is an ideology based on the belief that government should be in the hands of _____.

2. In modern times, traditional autocracies have been replaced by regimes of the _____ and the _____ that are called _____.

3. Some of the common features of totalitarian regimes include _____ against present society, hope for a _____ society, prescription for a lifestyle in _____ of life.

4. Totalitarian regimes maintain a _____ party through which the ideology is _____ _____; the leader or oligarchy _____ the ideology to the masses.

5. The two totalitarian ideologies of the right are _____, which originated in _____ in 19__; and _____, which arose in _____-_____ a decade later.

6. The principal elements of fascist ideology include: a_____ of reason, a denial of _____ _____, and behavior based on a code of _____.

7. In a fascist regime, the economy is divided into state-controlled associations of _____ and _____; the ultimate mediator is the _____.

F. CHAPTER OVERVIEW

Democracy, the ideology diametrically opposed to autocracy, is an **ideology, a philosophy, a theory, and a political system**. Among the **assumptions** and principles of democracy are: that the **individual** is **valuable** in addition to being free, rational, moral, equal, and in possession of certain rights. Another **central element** of democratic philosophy is the principle that the only **legitimate basis for rule is peoples' consent** to be ruled. Thus, the state is merely a trustee of the people and has no authority or purpose except as assigned by the people.

Capitalism is considered a **subideology**, or a blend of political and economic ideas that are mutually reinforcing. Classical capitalism is **based** on the ideas of Adam Smith who, in his **The Wealth of Nations** (1776) maintained a belief in the private ownership of property, in the existence of a profit motive, in the dynamics of a free market; and in the importance of competition. The private ownership of property is beneficial, according to Smith, first, because the power it creates is better in the hands of many individuals rather than concentrated in the state, and second, because the economic growth of the society is attained more easily if each individual uses personal incentive to get ahead. Smith also believed that the free market system worked smoothly, as if an "invisible hand" were directing it.

Classical capitalism has undergone many transformations, and today's economies are usually called **mixed economies** in which the government does interfere, competition has been diluted by the existence of private or state monopolies, and in which the **profit motive,** though still dominant, also can lead to bankruptcies and failures. In order to work perfectly, capitalism must exist in an environment of perfect equality of opportunity. But for a variety of reasons such equality of opportunity is difficult to attain; so nations with capitalistic mixed economies have adopted **welfare systems** to help those who are victimized by the system. But such systems are seldom completely successful.

Although socialism refers to an economic concept, **democratic socialism** is an ideology that rests on both economic and political assumptions. Its most fundamental assumption is that participation in political decision making should be extended to economic decision making. Thus, voters should be able to control their economic future as they do their political future. In all other re-spects, democratic socialism accepts and supports the democratic ideology, both in theory and in practice. Democratic **socialism** assumes that the **state** and its government are the **necessary instruments** through which people can achieve and maintain their objectives, some of which are: holding most **property in the name of the people**, especially all major **industries, utilities, and transpor-tation**; limiting the accumulation of private property; and **regulating the economy**.

The key difference between democratic **capitalism** and democratic **socialism** is the way **property is held** in a society. Democratic socialists argue that by ensuring everyone of economic security, they are making liberty possible for everyone. Democratic capitalists argue that only when property is held privately are people free to compete for rewards. Socialism attempts to bring together the best elements of Western civilization. The dilemma it faces is how to avoid the growth of the power of the state at the expense of individual freedom.

F. FILL IN THE BLANKS:

1. Some of the assumptions of democracy include: the_____ of the individual,
and that individuals are _____, _____, _____and in possession of specific _____.
2. A central element of the democratic philosophy is the principle that the only legitimate basis for rule is_____ _____to be ruled.
3. The state is merely a _____of the people and has no authority except as _____by the people.
4. Capitalism is a_____, a blend of_____ and _____ and _____ideas.
5. Classical capitalism is based on the ideas of _____who wrote _____ _____ __ _____in _____.

6. The principles of classical capitalism include: the ownership of _____,
the _____ motive, a _____ market, and _____.
7. Today's economies are called _____ because they include
government _____, a diluted form of _____, and a profit
motive that can lead to _____.
8. To work perfectly, capitalism should exist in an environment of _____
_____.
9. The most fundamental assumption of democratic socialism is that
_____ decision making should be extended to _____ decision making.
10. Socialism assumes that the instrument through which people attain their
goals is the _____ and its _____.
11. The key difference between democratic capitalism and democratic socialism
is the way _____ is held.

Terms to Remember

authoritarianism A type of autocracy (see below) in which power is held by an absolute monarch, dictator, or small elite. Power is limited to the political sphere.

autocracy An ideology directly opposed to democracy, in which government rests in the hands of one individual or group who holds supreme power over the people.

charismatic authority According to Max Weber, a type of authority based on the leadership of a person with charisma. A charismatic leader is thought to possess special gifts of a magnetic, fascinating, and extraordinary nature.

communism A political and economic ideology whose ultimate goal is total government control of the economy and total income redistribution, leading to the creation of a classless society.

democracy An ideology, philosophy, theory, and political system assuming the basic value of the individual, as well as his or her rationality, morality, equality, and possession of specific rights.

democratic capitalism A blend of political and economic ideology whose tenets include the private ownership of property, the profit motive, a free market economy, and competition. The function of government in this system is to ensure that the economic game is played fairly.

democratic socialism A blend of political and economic ideology whose chief assumption is that participation in political decision making should be extended to economic decision making. The function of the government in this system is to control and guide the economy for the benefit of the voters who elected it.

fascism A totalitarian ideology of the right that became prominent in various nations beginning in Italy under Benito Mussolini.

ideology A system of ideas, values, beliefs, and attitudes that a society or groups within a society share and accept as true.

legal-rational authority According to Weber, a type of authority accepted by members of society because it is based on rational methods and laws and is exerted for their benefit.

nation A culture group residing within the territory of a political state.

nationalism The ideology behind the nation-state. A set of beliefs about the superiority of one's own nation and a defense of its interest above all others.

nazism The German version of fascism that flourished under the leadership of Adolf Hitler.

politics The forces that make up and direct the government of the state, its policies, and its actions.

power The probability that one individual in a social relationship will carry out his or her own will despite resistance. The ability of one person or group to direct the behavior of another person or group in a desired direction, under the ultimate, though not always obvious, threat of force.

rule of law A constitutional principle holding that those in public authority derive, maintain, and exercise their powers on the basis of specific laws, and not on the basis of their personal power.

totalitarianism A type of autocracy of the left or of the right, characterized by a totalist ideology, a single party, a government-controlled secret police, and a monopoly over mass communications, weapons, and the economy by the ruling elite.

traditional authority According to Weber, authority that is based on reverence for tradition.

State The abstract embodiment, or the symbol, of the political institution.

TEST YOUR KNOWLEDGE. HOW MUCH DO YOU RECALL?
MULTIPLE CHOICE QUESTIONS:

1. A system of ideas, values, beliefs, and attitudes shared by members of a society and accepted as true by them is a(n):
    a. doctrine
    b. religion
    c. philosophy
    d. ideology

2. One of the basic assumptions of the ideology of democracy is:
    a. the importance of the collectivity
    b. the value of the individual
    c. equality of results
    d. the pursuit of happiness

3. Autocracy may be defined as:
    a. the ideology most directly opposed to democracy
    b. the ideology that holds that government should be in the hands of the people
    c. a corollary of democracy
    d. a precursor of democracy

4. Totalitarian regimes:
    a. are the equivalent of the autocracies of the past
    b. can exist within democracies
    c. are kinds of autocracies based on modern technology and mass legitimization
    d. are short-lived dictatorships

5. The goal of communism was:
    a. to prohibit any evidence of capitalist market activity
    b. to reverse the class system of societies
    c. private ownership of the means of production
    d. total income redistribution and ultimately a classless society

6. In most societies, ownership of property takes one of three forms:
    a. restricted, guarded, and private
    b. esthetic, visible, tangible
    c. communal, private, public
    d. ambiguous, hermetic, contraceptive

7. What does one call property owned by the state in the name of the people?

a. public
b. private
c. common-law
d. communal

8. The "invisible hand" refers to:
    a. a feature of Adam Smith's Wealth of Nations
    b. the belief in God exhibited by the Puritans
    c. the fact that prayer results in help
    d. a belief in ghosts prevalent in the early Middle Ages

9. "Laissez-faire":
    a. has nothing to do with economic theory
    b. is the rallying cry of the Gay Liberation Movement
    c. was Karl Marx's exhortation to the workers of the world
    d. is the French word Adam Smith used to mean that government should keep its hands off the economy

10. The private ownership of property was deemed beneficial to the society because it:
    a. diffused power
    b. used the incentive motive
    c. was the American way
    d. only a and b

11. The fundamental assumption of democratic socialism is that:
    a. participation in political decision making should be extended to religious leaders
    b. the Socialist party must be in command of the economy
    c. participation in political decision making should be extended to economic decision making
    d. it is not necessary for everyone in a society to work

12. Which is **not** a characteristic of the fascist ideology?
    a. Distrust of reason
    b. Concern with basic equality of humankind
    c. Code of behavior based on violence
    d. Government by elite

13. The "dialectic" is a tool of analysis associated with the work of:
    a. Karl Marx
    b. Adam Smith
    c. Benito Mussolini
    d. Adolf Hitler

14. In its most dogmatic aspect, the communist ideology focused on the following goals:
    a. abolition of all private property
    b. class warfare
    c. the dictatorship of the proletariat
    d. all of the above
    e. none of the above

15. Karl Marx predicted that the revolution would occur in:
    a. the United States
    b. Russia
    c. Germany
    d. Great Britain

16. One mistake Marx made was that he underestimated the workers':
    a. ignorance
    b. nationalism
    c. poverty
    d. laziness

17. Political ideology deals with:
    a. matters of ruler selection and principles of rule
    b. parties
    c. economics
    d. none of the above

18. MacIver believed that the main function of political ideology (myth complex was:
    a. making people feel free
    b. secure the will of the people
    c. give legitimate authority to the government in power
    d. fool the people some of the time

19. "The probability that one actor within a social relationship will be in a position to carry out his own will despite resistance" is a definition of:
    a. the top echelons of management
    b. leadership abilities
    c. power
    d. stardom in the rock music industry

20. Legal-rational authority is characteristic of:
    a. homogeneous societies
    b. traditional, agrarian societies
    c. urban industrial, developed societies
    d. totalitarian societies

173

21. The difference between government and state is that:
   a. government is a symbol and state is the process
   b. government is a process that includes the people who exercise political power
   c. the state is an abstract symbol of the political institution
   d. both b and c

22. The most important function of government is to:
   a. provide social welfare
   b. implement social control
   c. exercise total control
   d. regulate human life in society

23. The basic components of the state include all but which of the following?
   a. Territory
   b. Population
   c. Armed services
   d. Sovereignty

24. The functionalist school maintains that the state:
   a. protects the rights of the privileged
   b. is on the way out
   c. is an extension of the "state of nature"
   d. is a human invention necessary to maintain order

25. Pivotal institutions include:
   a. property, warfare, and the law
   b. the family, religion, and government
   c. faith, hope, and charity
   d. insane asylums, prisons, and public schools

26. Hitler led the German people by emotional speeches. He derived his authority from:
   a. God
   b. the law
   c. the Bible
   d. personal charisma

27. Functionalists approach the state as a tool to:
   a. maintain order
   b. protect the privileged few
   c. protect private property
   d. maintain the state of nature

28. Conflict theorists see the state's functions as:
    a. protecting the interest of the ruling elite only
    b. helping the poor and homeless
    c. bringing peace to its citizens
    d. directing the economy

29. Marx believed that the state would vanish when:
    a. the elite would work toward the good of the masses
    b. the lion would lie down with the lamb
    c. social classes ceased to exist
    d. all societies became capitalist

30. "My country, right or wrong" is an example of:
    a. nationalism
    b. legal-rational thinking
    c. an internationalist world view
    d. a reasoned approach to peace

31. A person affected by nationalism:
    a. identifies with a state's culture
    b. shares a state's interests and goals
    c. displays feelings of ethnocentrism
    d. all of the above
    e. none of the above

ANSWERS TO FILL IN THE BLANKS

A. 1. social order
    2. group, social control
    3. power
    4. social control
    5. institutionalized
    6. power
    7. moral control
    8. political control
    9. when, how, whom
    10. protects, maintains, regulates

B. 1. power
    2. in spite of resistance
    3. rewards, coercion, influence
    4. state, government
    5. authority
    6. legitimate

7. right and proper
8. authority
9. coercion
10. traditional, legal-rational, charismatic

C. 1. process, group of people
    2. abstract, symbol
    3. permanent, temporary
    4. population, territory, government, sovereignty
    5. Thomas Hobbes, John Locke

D. 1. systems, rational, intelligible, logical
    2. sets of attitudes
    3. picture, should be
    4. times of crisis, dominant, unacceptable
    5. comprehensive, abstract, reductionist
    6. justification to government, structure, mission and purpose
    7. who will govern, selected, principles
    8. persuade, opposing
    9. retaining, reforming, abolishing
    10. monolithic, socialized, conflicting

E. 1. person, group, power
    2. right, left, totalitarian
    3. revolt, better, in all spheres
    4. single, kept alive, interprets
    5. fascism, Italy, 1922, nazism, Germany
    6. distrust, basic equality, violence
    7. capital, labor, state

F. 1. value, free, moral, rational, rights
    2. people's consent
    3. trustee, assigned
    4. subideology, political, economic
    5. Adam Smith, The Wealth of Nations, 1776
    6. private property, profit, free, competition
    7. mixed, intervention, competition, failure
    8. equal opportunity
    9. political, economic
    10. state, government
    11. property

ANSWERS TO MULTIPLE CHOICE QUESTIONS:

1. d
2. b
3. a
4. c
5. d
6. c
7. a
8. a
9. d
10. d
11. c
12. b
13. a
14. d
15. c
16. b
17. a
18. c
19. d
20. d
21. b
22. a
23. b
24. b
25. a
26. d
27. a
28. a
29. c
30. a
31. d

CHAPTER 15: THE GOVERNMENT

OF THE UNITED STATES OF AMERICA

In this chapter, you will learn

1. the historical sequence in the establishment of American political institutions;
2. about the implications of the executive branch;
3. the weaknesses of the legislative branch;
4. the functions of the judicial branch;
5. the importance of limited government.

TOPICAL OUTLINE

I. AMERICAN POLITICAL INSTITUTIONS
    A. The Constitutional Convention
        1. Goals of the Constitutional Convention
        2. What Is A Constitution?

II. THE CONSTITUTION OF THE UNITED STATES

III. FEDERALISM
    A. How Federalism Has Worked
    B. Trend Toward Centralization
    C. Impact of Federal Government

IV. SEPARATION OF POWERS
    A. How Checks and Balances Work
    B. Criticism of the Separation of Powers

V. THE PRESIDENCY: THE EXECUTIVE BRANCH
    A. The Nature of the Presidency
        1. The Roles of the President
        2. The Presidency: The Person and the Office

VI. CONGRESS: THE LEGISLATIVE BRANCH
    A. The Issue of Representation
        1. Congressional Organization
        2. Congressional Committees
        3. Seniority Rule
        4. The Subordinate Role of Congress

VII. THE SUPREME COURT: THE JUDICIAL BRANCH
    A. The Court System

1. Functions of the Judicial System

VIII. THE IMPORTANCE OF LIMITED GOVERNMENT

A. CHAPTER OVERVIEW

With the **exception** of political **parties**, all of the political institutions of the United States were **conceived** and delineated at the **Constitutional Convention of 1787**. It has been charged that the originators of the Constitution met to preserve the interests of their social class--propertied landowners-but the opinion now prevails that their chief **concern** was really to create a **government** that would **survive** and be **workable** and still serve the interests of all groups in society.

Constitutions are instruments for establishing a framework for government. They **limit the power of the government** by stating the boundaries of its authority. They provide **specific procedures** for governmental **action**, and, by implication, **forbid** other action. Thus, the governed are guaranteed protection against possible arbitrary actions of the governors. The true ruler in such a framework is the law. This **"rule of law"** is an important principle of constitutionality. It holds that those in public authority **derive, maintain, and exercise** their powers on the basis of **laws** specifically drawn up. The four major constitutional principles of American government are: **federalism, separation of powers** and **checks and balances; judicial supremacy** and limited **government**.

Federalism may be defined as a **system** of distributing political power between a **central**, national government and the governments of the geographical regions into which the nation is divided. The allocation of power is outlined in the Constitution and may be altered only by a **constitutional amendment**. In theory, the federal system brings government closer to the people because state governments are not subordinate to the central government.

But federalism necessitates a vast **bureaucracy** in which various agencies quibble about authority and resources. There are also **inequities** in the way some state programs are administered, leading to the trend of letting the national government assume a larger share of responsibility. The principle of **separation of powers** is also prescribed by the Constitution. It provides for the **legislative, executive, and judicial** functions to be divided among three separate branches of government, one to **formulate and enact laws**, another to see that the laws are **carried out**, and a third to determine whether the laws are in **agreement** with the Constitution. Each branch is directly involved in the workings of the other two through the process of **checks and balances**. While the principle is criticized because the system is often cumbersome, unwieldy, and slow, the concern was for power to be shared and not allowing it to become concentrated in one branch.

A. FILL IN THE BLANKS:

1. Only_____ _____were not conceived and outlined at the _____ _____in 1787.

2. Constitutions are instruments for establishing a _____   for
_____.

3. Constitutions_ _____the power of the government,   provide
_____for government action, and they forbid other actions by
_____.

4. The most important principle of constitutionality is the_____ __ _____.

5. The four principles of the American Constitution are:
_____,_____ _____,_____ _____,
and_____ _____.

6. Federalism is a system of _____political power between the
_____government and the governments of the regions into which the
nation is divided.

7. The allocation of power is outlined in the _____and may be altered
only by _____amendment.

8. The disadvantages of federalism include a vast _____and the
_____with which state programs are administered.

9. The principle that the legislative, executive, and judicial functions of
government be separated is called_____ __ _____.

10. Each branch of government is directly involved in the working of the other
two through the process of_____ ____ _____.

B. CHAPTER OVERVIEW

There were no models for the Constitutional Convention to follow regarding an **executive branch** or the office of the president. What finally emerged as the office of the **chief executive** included these features: one chief executive; a four-year-term that could be terminated only by death or impeachment; the electoral base to be independent of Congress; and some constitutional powers independent of Congress, the electors, the people, and the states. As for the **roles** of the chief executive, they are: chief of state, chief legislator, chief administrator, chief diplomat or foreign policy maker, party leader, and commander-in-chief of the armed forces.

The delegates also devised a system of government that included a **popular representative assembly**, the House of Representatives. The House was to be the **forum for the people** of the entire nation, while the **Senate** was to have the same purpose for the states and minorities. The Constitution leaves the manner of election of representatives up to the individual states. The state legislatures chose to divide the states into **congressional districts** for election purposes. Districts must be reapportioned every ten years after the census. Representation has not been perfect: studies have shown that members of Congress do not necessarily represent the feelings of most of their constituents, especially in the sphere of foreign relations and social welfare. Congressional **organization**, with older members clinging to **tradition** and demanding deference, and the powerful influence exerted by some committees, seems to partially explain the ineffectiveness of Congress which is felt most acutely in the areas of foreign relations and military affairs. Most policy proposals tend to **originate in the executive branch** and from military and industrial pressure groups.

The **Supreme Court** was meant to represent a final bulwark against **majority tyranny** as well as a check on the representational aspect of Congress and the independent aspect of the presidency. **Judicial review** is the ability to judge the constitutionality of presidential and Congressional acts, as well as that of state legislation. Because of the federal type of government, the judicial system that has arisen in the United States is quite **complex**. It includes 50 sets of state judicial hierarchies, in addition to the federal judicial hierarchy. State courts, while not inferior to federal courts, have jurisdiction in cases arising out of state constitutions and state statutes, as well as out of the common law of each state. The judicial power to interpret and apply statutes to specific cases is, however, a lawmaking power itself. Judges possess a degree of choice which may be as great as that of other legislative bodies.

The principle of **limited government** is **basic to constitutionalism** because in the democratic tradition the purpose of a constitution is to limit the power of government. The very structure and processes of government express this principle. Further limitations on government are **embodied** in the **Bill of Rights** and particularly in the First Amendment.

B. FILL IN THE BLANKS:

1. The executive branch, as finally outlined by the Constitutional Convention, includes these features: one_____ _____, a _____-____ term, an_ _____electoral base, and some _____constitutional powers.
2. Among the roles of the president are: chief _____, chief _____, chief _____, chief _____,party _____, and _____ - __ _____of the armed forces.
3. The House of Representatives was intended to be a forum for the _____ _____.
4. According to the Constitution, representatives are elected in the manner chosen by the _____.
5. State legislatures divided states into_____ _____for elections.

6. Although constitutionally Congress had the potential for power, in reality its role has been _____ to the executive branch.

7. Policy proposals that do not originate in the executive, do so   from _____and_____ _____groups.

8. The Supreme Court was intended as a check on the_____ aspect of Congress and the _____aspect of the presidency.

9. Judicial review is the ability to judge the _____of presidential and Congressional _____as well as that of _____ _____.

10. The judicial system of the United States is very _____; state courts have jurisdiction in cases arising out of _____constitutions and statutes, as well as out of the _____ _____of their state.

11. The judicial power to interpret and apply statutes is a _____power in itself.

TERMS TO REMEMBER

checks and balances: The method resulting from the principle of separation of powers in which each branch of government is directly and indirectly involved in the workings of the other branches.

concurrent powers: Powers shared by the central government and the state governments, according to the specifications of the Constitution of the United States.

constitutional government: A government that is subject to limitations and that operates in accordance with general rules rather than arbitrarily. The existence of a constitution places a system of effective restraints on political power.

federalism: A form of government in which power is distributed between the central and regional units, each retaining sovereignty in specified spheres.

house rules committee: The group with the power to determine the specific time allotted for the debate of important legislation. This is one of the most important committees in the House of Representatives.

implied powers: Powers that are assumed by inference from the delegated powers granted to the central government, according to the Constitution of the United States.

judicial review: The power exercised by the Supreme Court to invalidate presidential, congressional, and state legislative action that it deems contrary to the Constitution of the United States.

Marbury vs. Madison: The case that established the principle of judicial review.

residual or reserved powers: Powers reserved for the states of the people, according to the Constitution of the United States.

rule of law: A constitutional principle holding that those in public authority derive, maintain, and exercise their powers on the basis of specific laws, and not on the basis of their personal power.

seniority rule: A principle strictly adhered to in Congress by which committee chairpersonships and memberships are determined by the years of service in Congress and on the particular committee.

separation of powers: An arrangement prescribed by the Constitution in which three separate branches of government are entrusted with the legislative, executive, and judicial functions.

HOW MUCH DO YOU RECALL? TEST YOUR KNOWLEDGE

MULTIPLE CHOICE QUESTIONS

1. The system of distributing political power between a central national government and the governments of the geographical regions of the nation is called:
   a. confederacy
   b. federalism
   c. centralism
   d. unitarianism

2. The chief reason that Congress is so ineffective is:
   a. that the Constitution delegates it so little power
   b. a result of the gradual emergence of the Supreme Court as a legislative body
   c. the development of the power of state governments
   d. the traditional organization of the legislative branch

3. Which is not a restraint imposed on the United States government?
   a. Presidential supremacy
   b. Federalism
   c. Separation of power
   d. Checks and balances

4. Which is not a presidential role?
   a. Chief Justice
   b. commander-in-chief of armed forces

c. chief diplomat

d. party leader

5. Congressional representation is based on:
    a. single-member constituency system
    b. proportional representation
    c. parliamentary system
    d. only b and c

6. Judicial review by the Supreme Court is based on:
    a. explicit statements in the Constitution
    b. the Marbury v. Madison decision
    c. an act of Congress
    d. the First Amendment to the Constitution

7. The favorable evaluation of our presidents is based on:
    a. the caretaker role
    b. strict adherence to the written Constitution
    c. dynamic political leadership
    d. the teflon principle

8. Congressional members, in reality:
    a. represent local elites
    b. have little knowledge of what constituents want
    c. are interested in local welfare
    d. all of the above

9. Some state powers are inferred from the powers specifically delegated by the Constitution to the central government. These are called:
    a. inferred powers
    b. residual powers
    c. implied powers
    d. reserved powers

10. The federal system has worked particularly well in:
    a. large-sized countries with regional differences
    b. small, homogeneous countries
    c. small urban industrial countries
    d. large homogeneous single-religion countries

11. The federal system is contrasted with a(n):
    a. unitary system
    b. confederate system
    c. catholic system
    d. none of the above

e. **BOTH** unitary **and** confederate systems

12. Federalism may be defined as a system of:
    a. concurrent powers
    b. central power
    c. wholesale power
    d. regional power

13. The principle of separation of power had been discussed by the following political thinkers prior to their incorporation into the Constitution:
    a. Thomas Jefferson and Benjamin Franklin
    b. Adam Smith and John Maynard Keynes
    c. John Locke and Charles Montesquieu
    d. Alexis de Tocqueville and Jean-Jacques Rousseau

14. The President fills all but which of the following roles?
    a. Chief of state
    b. Speaker of the House
    c. Chief administrator
    d. Commander-in-chief of the Armed Forces

15. Which of the following is true?
    a. The president, Supreme Court Justices, and all members of Congress are elected by popular vote
    b. Senate members are elected but the members of the House are appointed by the president
    c. Each branch of government is brought to office by a different constituency
    d. Supreme Court Justices are appointed by the Senate and voted in by the House

16. When did the United States government begin to function as a cohesive unit?
    a. At the signing of the Declaration of Independence
    b. At the Constitutional Convention of 1787
    c. At the signing of the Articles of Confederation
    d. At the Inauguration of George Washington in 1789

17. What were the goals of the Constitutional Convention?
    a. To preserve the status quo
    b. To form a government that would serve the interests of all groups in the society
    c. To insure the power of the small farmers
    d. To diminish the power of a strong central government

ANSWERS TO FILL IN THE BLANKS:

A. 1. political parties, Constitutional Convention
    2. framework, government
    3. limit, procedures, implication
    4. rule of law
    5. federalism, separation of powers, judicial supremacy, limited government
    6. distributing, central
    7. Constitution, constitutional
    8. bureaucracy, inequity
    9. separation of powers
    10. checks and balances

B. 1. chief executive, four-year, independent, independent
    2. of state, legislator, administrator, diplomat, party leader, commander-in-chief
    3. entire nation
    4. states
    5. Congressional Districts
    6. subordinate
    7. military, industrial pressure
    8. representational, independent
    9. constitutionality, acts, state legislatures
    10. complex, state, common law
    11. lawmaking

ANSWERS TO MULTIPLE CHOICE QUESTIONS:

1. b
2. d
3. a
4. a
5. b
6. b
7. c
8. d
9. c
10. a
11. e
12. a
13. c
14. b

5. c
6. b
7. b

187

CHAPTER 16: WE, THE PEOPLE

DEMOCRACY IN ACTION

In this chapter, you will learn

1. how the ideology of democracy is interpreted and how it translates in practical terms when applied to a political system;
2. which model of the location of political power--pluralism or elitism--best fits the United States;
3. the nature, functions, negative and positive facets of interest groups (including lobbies and PACs);
4. the nature, functions, purpose, weaknesses, or strengths of political parties;
5. that voting is the chief form of political expression;
6. who does and does not vote in the United States;
7. the meaning of public opinion;
8. the importance of the mass media in the political process.

TOPICAL OUTLINE

I. AMERICAN DEMOCRACY

II. HOW IS AMERICA GOVERNED
    A. Elitism
    B. Pluralism
        1. Conflict and Consensus
        2. A Realistic Democracy

III. INTEREST GROUPS
    A. Functions of Interest Groups
    B. Formation and Growth of Interest Groups
        1. Lobbyists
        2. PACs
    C. Shortcomings of Interest Groups

IV. POLITICAL PARTIES
    A. Purpose of Political Parties
    B. The Functions of Political Parties
    C. Features of the American Party System
    D. Winner Take All
    E. Third Parties
    F. The Party System in Decline
    G. Realignment or Dealignment?

A. CHAPTER OVERVIEW

In the **classic conception of democracy**, individuals should be able to participate in the decisions of government directly. Participation is to be achieved through **majority rule**, but always respecting the **rights of minorities**. In a large and **heterogeneous** society, such direct participation is not possible. Yet, to make decisions binding on the entire society is to have the ultimate power to rule. If not the people, then who has this power in the United States? There are two **opposing schools of thought** on how power is distributed in this society.

According to **political pluralism**, or broker rule, power is diffused among numerous interest groups, and is not concentrated in a singly place. According to **elitism**, power is held by a limited number of individuals or groups. In reality, both views are probably correct, and the truth lies somewhere in the middle.

According to subscribers to both views, Americans are too apathetic, ill informed, and self interested to participate in the kind of system that democratic ideology prescribes. The **pluralists**, however, state that those in power are **responsive** to the people, even though the latter may be uninterested; so that while government is run by an elite, that elite is approved by the people. The **elitists** maintain that an apparent consensus is brought about by an elite which **manipulates** the masses through mass communication. **Public policy**, according to elitists, **reflects** not the demands of the masses, but the **values** of the elite.

There is disagreement also over the interplay of **conflict** and **consensus** in society, especially over which of the two predominates in the United States. Pluralists tend to belong to the consensus school of thought, according to which conflict takes place within a general framework of consensus. Elitists are likely to agree with the conflict school of thought, believing that ultimately, it is **force** that binds a society together. **Consensus is necessary for democracy** to work; but conflict keeps the system from stifling diversity and dissent. The right to

189

organize an **opposition** for the purpose of gaining access to power in the process of decision making is a **fundamental element of democracy**. Such opposition usually takes the form of political **parties** whose primary purpose is to gain control of government and take on the responsibility for conducting its affairs.

A. FILL IN THE BLANKS

1. According to classical democracy, the power to make decisions binding on the society should belong to the _____.
2. Direct political participation is _____ in a large   and _____ society.
3. There are two opposing schools of thought on how power is distributed in this society: _____ and _____.
4. Power is diffused among numerous interest groups, according to the

_____.
5. Power is concentrated in the hands of a limited number of individuals or groups, according to the _____.
6. A fundamental democratic right is to organize an _____.
7. In order for democracy to work, both _____ and _____ are necessary.

B. CHAPTER OVERVIEW

Among the functions of political parties are: to **determine and define** the ideals and interests of the people, clarifying them as issues and ideologies; **to providing** the **personnel** necessary to run the government; to act as the loyal opposition (criticizing the party in power); and to educate the electorate in political matters. The American party system is a **two-party system**, and the two parties are not based on any particular doctrine or ideology. Rather, within each party there is a vast **variety of opinions** on specific issues and on how to achieve the goals of the society. American parties are **decentralized**, with diffused control. Finally, American parties are **durable**. Party organization consists of formal leadership, lower-echelon party activists, informal power holders (financial contributors), and passive voters. A frequent criticism of political parties is that their internal structure is undemocratic; but it is argued that as long as leaders remain responsive, internal democracy is unimportant.

What all agree should be reformed is the area of **campaign expenditures** and the time spent campaigning. Funds for electoral campaigns are provided by party activists who spend much time and energy on this activity although parties and their candidates depend on a few large donations from a small percentage of wealthy citizens. The Corrupt Practices Act prohibits any person from donating more than $5000 to any one political organization and forbids corporations, trade unions, and national banks to contribute. The law has produced an unintended side effect in the popularity of **Political Action Committees** (PACs) which have been so successful that more money has been poured into campaigns than ever before.

One can participate in political decision making by joining interest groups. **Interest groups** are **coalitions** of individuals with similar attitudes and interests who attempt to influence public policy. **Public policy** is that which government does or does not do. Interest groups resemble political parties, but differ from them in the manner of pursuing their goals. The principal activity of interest groups is lobbying, or attempting to influence public officials into passing legislation beneficial to their members.

B. FILL IN THE BLANKS:

1. The primary purpose of political parties is to_____ _____ of government and take responsibility for _____its affairs.
2. Some of the functions of political parties include: _____and _____the interests of the people; providing _____to run the government; and acting as the

_____ _____.
3. Characteristics of the American party system include: it is a____ _____ _____; the parties are not based on a particular _____; and the parties are _____.
4. Party organizations consists of _____, _____, _____, and ordinary _____.
5. A criticism of the parties is that their internal structure is often _____.
6. There is agreement on the need to reform _____ _____.
7. Funds for electoral campaigns are provided by _____ _____, and especially by a few _____ _____from wealthy citizens.
8. One individual cannot donate more than _____ to any one political organization.
9. _____, _____ _____, and _____ _____ are forbidden to contribute to political organizations.
10. An unintended side effect of the Corrupt Practices Act has been the formation of ____ _____ _____, which have poured even more money into political campaigns.
11. Individuals can participate in political decision-making by joining _____

_____.
12. Coalitions of individuals with similar attitudes and interests who attempt to influence public policy is a definition of____ _____.
13. Public policy is that which government _____or does___ ____.
14. The principal function of interest groups is _____.

C. CHAPTER OVERVIEW

In studying voter behavior, social scientists have uncovered that there is a cynical **lack of faith** in democratic processes and in the right of some people to self government. In addition, democratic principles and values evoke a wide **consensus** when referred to in general terms, but not when the principles are applied to specific issues. There is also a **greater commitment** to democratic principles among the **leaders**, the politically active, well-educated elites **than among the masses** of people.

Although the United States was one of the first nations in the world to extend universal adult suffrage, only about 60 percent of its citizens vote in presidential elections. The **lowest voting record** occurs among unskilled workers with inadequate educations, and the **young**, the **underprivileged**, and **minority** groups. The reverse tends to be true of the college-educated, professional--managerial, and white-collar workers. The feeling among the politically alienated is that conventional political participation is meaningless. Gaps in information lead to contradictory opinions, and eventually to irrational voting. **Voting** is acting on a political opinion. But the first amendment also guarantees each individual the right to have a **political opinion**. Public and political opinion are frequently used interchangeably, but they are not the same. Public opinion is the totality of opinions expressed by members of a community on any issue. **Political opinion** is the totality of opinions expressed by these same individuals on political issues alone.

Commentators in the communication media must select the events to be reported. This choice brings the public dangerously close to receiving propaganda instead of news, and to the selling of candidates and issues.

C. FILL IN THE BLANKS:

1. American voters appear to have a cynical _____ of faith in the _____ process.
2. There is consensus on democratic principles when they are presented in_____ _____.
3. There is greater commitment to democratic principles among   the _____, the politically _____, and the_____ _____than among the masses.
4. Only about _____ of the people vote in presidential elections.
5. The lowest voting record belongs to the _____, _____, _____, and _____.
6. Those who vote in greatest proportion tend to be_____ _____-___,_____ _____, and _____-_____workers.

7. The politically alienated believe that _____ _____
_____ is meaningless.
8. The First Amendment guarantees Americans the right to hold
a_____ _____.
9. Political opinion is the _____of opinions held by individuals on
_____issues alone.
10. There is danger in the mass media of communication because
commentators must _____what news to report, thus   inviting
_____.

TERMS TO REMEMBER

democratic pluralism: An interpretation of how the American political system works. This interpretation assumes that there are multiple centers of power, creating a situation in which political power is fragmented and diffused.

interest groups: Coalitions of individuals with similar interests who compete with one another for their share of political power, attempting to influence legislation in their favor.

lobbying: The principal activity of interest groups, consisting of attempts to influence public officials to pass legislation beneficial to the group or the people it represents.

majoritarian model of democracy: The classical model of democracy in which the statement "government by the people" is interpreted as meaning that the majority of the people make all government decisions directly.

party platform: A general statement of party positions and policies.

plural elites: Groups with diffused power and leadership roles, the representatives of different segments of the population to whom they are responsible through elections, interest groups, and partisan competition.

political opinion: The totality of opinions expressed by members of a community on political issues alone.

politics: The forces that make up and direct the government of the state, its policies, and its actions. Also, the institution that makes the decisions about "who gets what, when, and how" in society.

protest groups: Pressure groups characterized by protesting of certain governmental actions or inactions and calling attention to their grievances by such means as marches, sit-ins, demonstrations, and acts of civil disobedience.

public policy: That which government does or does not do.

ruling elite: A group composed of representatives of corporate, financial, military, and governmental interests who--according to some social scientists--make all the relevant decisions in the nation, irrespective of the wishes of the population at large.

HOW MUCH DO YOU RECALL? TEST YOUR KNOWLEDGE

MULTIPLE CHOICE QUESTIONS

1. One of the chief tenets of democratic ideology is that:
    a. popular participation must be representative
    b. the welfare of the community comes before the individual
    c. the individual has a major voice in public decisions
    d. the views of the minority have the same weight as those of the majority

2. Popular participation must be representative because:
    a. the size of the nation does not permit personal participation
    b. the ill and housebound cannot go to the polls
    c. not all people are acquainted with the issues
    d. many persons cannot pay the poll tax

3. The founders intended popular participation in government to be achieved through:
    a. the rule of elites
    b. majority rule with respect for rights of minorities
    c. rule by committee
    d. rule by minority coalitions

4. What does it mean to govern?
    a. To govern is to have won the election for president.
    b. It is to have the power to make decisions binding on the whole society.
    c. To govern is to be in charge of the military.
    d. The idea of governing died with the monarchy.

5. C. Wright Mills included in the political elite:
    a. the corporate rich
    b. the military upper echelon

c. the political directorate
d. all of the above

6. According to pluralism, power:
a. is held by one individual or a junta
b. is concentrated in the hands of a few
c. is diffused among numerous interest groups
d. belongs to the people

7. Elitism is a school of thought whose premise is that power:
a. is diffused in society
b. is held by the proletariat
c. is limited to a few
d. is shared only when issues are minor
e. both c and d

8. The basic purpose of political parties is to:
a. provide the "loyal opposition"
b. gain control of government and take on the responsibility for conducting its affairs
c. represent the interests of the electorate
d. build a platform

9. "Realist democracy" states that:
a. new social groups can become elites
b. the elites present a consensus on basic democratic beliefs
c. elites compete and rule through shifting coalitions
d. all of the above

10. One of the criticisms of political parties is that:
a. they tend to influence public policy
b. they are unconstitutional
c. their purpose is to seize power illegitimately
d. their methods of campaigning involve too much time and expense

11. Which of the following is **not** true of PACs?
a. PACs are created by presidential appointment
b. PACs are established by interest groups
c. PACs can donate money to any campaign they choose
d. PACs are viewed by some as greater dangers than campaign contributors

12. Interest groups:
a. address the overall interests of America

b. represent the ideologies of their members
c. have weakened the American party system
d. are accountable to the voting public

13. The American party system is said to be in decline because:
a. members of Congress vote straight party lines
b. the Democratic party controls two branches of government
c. voters split tickets and candidates run independently of their party's counsel
d. PACs have replaced wealthy individuals as primary donors to individual candidates

14. The percentage of the American electorate which votes in local elections is:
a. about the same as for the national elections
b. around 10 percent
c. about 50 percent
d. less than 5 percent

15. The "free-rider" problem refers to:
a. persons receiving free medical services for which they could afford to pay
b. political patronage
c. persons who refuse to join interest groups, but who still benefit from the successes of the interest group
d. voters claiming to have voted for the winning candidate when they did not

15. The person who warned of the dangers of the "military-industrial complex" was:
a. General Colin Powell
b. General Patton
c. General Eisenhower
d. General Shelton

16. An oligarchy is:
a. rule by a few
b. rule by many
c. rule by pluralities
d. the same as anarchy

17. "Broker rule" is a term associated with:
a. Wall Street
b. sports management

c. pluralism
d. elitism

18. Some of the functions of interest groups include:
     a. informing the public
     b. helping legislators
     c. acting to identify public needs
     d. all of the above
     e. none of the above

19. In what way can interest groups pose a threat to democracy?
     a. They may act as spies for foreign governments.
     b. They are not elected by the people.
     c. They may stand for unpopular ideas.
     d. They may try to corrupt our young people.

ANSWERS TO FILL IN THE BLANKS:

A.   l. people
       2. impossible, heterogeneous
       3. pluralism, elitism
       4. pluralists
       5. elitists
       6. opposition
       7. conflict, consensus

B.   1. take control, conducting
       2. determining and defining, personnel, loyal opposition
       3. two-party system, doctrine, durable
       4. formal leadership, party activists, financial contributors, and voters
       5. undemocratic
       6. campaign spending
       7. party activists, large donations
       8. $5,000
       9. corporations, trade unions, national banks
       10. Political Action Committees
       11. Interest groups
       12. Interest groups
       13. Does or does not do
       14. lobbying

C.   1. lack, democratic
       2. general terms

3. leaders, active, well educated
4. 60 percent
5. young, unskilled, undereducated, minorities
6. college-educated, professional-managerial, white-collar workers
7. conventional political participation
8. political opinion
9. totality, political
10. select, propaganda

ANSWERS TO MULTIPLE CHOICE QUESTIONS:

1. c
2. a
3. b
4. b
5. d
6. c
7. e
8. b
9. d
10. d
11. a
12. c
13. c
14. b
15. c
16. c
17. a
18. c
19. d
20. b

CHAPTER 17: THE ECONOMY

CONCEPTS AND HISTORY

In this chapter, you will learn:

1. the purpose and functions of the economy as an institution;
2. the concepts that economists use in describing economies;
3. the historical development of Western economies;
4. the nature and features of the American economy in its historical framework;
5. the characteristics of the corporate hierarchy;
6. about the development of a global economic system.

TOPICAL OUTLINE

I. THE ECONOMY AS AN INSTITUTION
    A. Economic Decision Making
    B. Basic Elements of the Economy
    C. Factors of Production
    D. Economic Choices and Opportunity Costs
    E. Limits to Output: Production possibilities frontier
    F. Specialization of Labor
    G. Trade, barter, and money

II. CONTEMPORARY ECONOMIC SYSTEMS: HOW CHOICES ARE MADE

III. WESTERN ECONOMIES IN HISTORICAL PERSPECTIVE
    A. The Birth of Capitalism

IV. ASPECTS OF INDUSTRIAL CAPITALISM
    A. The Corporate Form of Industrial Organization
    B. From Competition to Advertising

V. DIVERSIFICATION AND MULTINATIONALISM

VI. THE NATURE OF WORK IN THE INDUSTRIAL SOCIETY
    A. Shifting Sectors
    B. Professionalization

VII. THE CORPORATE BUREAUCRACY
    A. The Executive
        1. Anxiety

A. CHAPTER OVERVIEW

To sustain life, people need a constant supply of **food**, sufficient **shelter**, and **clothing** to protect them from extreme temperatures. These elements, unlike air or water which are also needed to survive, are **scarce** and require effort to obtain. The institution of the **economy** consists of those patterns of behavior which revolve around obtaining the scarce resources necessary for survival. The "economy," then, is an abstract concept representing **relationships** among people and groups of people who **behave** according to specific, traditional patterns in order to achieve the goal of survival.

In the face of the perpetual problem of scarcity of resources, each society must ask itself the following questions: **What should** be produced, and in what quantities? **How should** it be produced with the greatest efficiency? **For whom should** these commodities be produced? In short, decisions must be made about the **production, distribution and exchange**, and consumption of goods and services. These decisions are made differently in different societies. Some rely only on **custom and tradition**; others decide by the **command** of a ruler or body of representatives; others still reach these decisions as a result of the functioning of a **market system** dependent on supply and demand, prices, profits, and losses. Most modern economies use a variety of these methods of decision making. These decisions are analyzed within the context of **microeconomics**, an area of the discipline which is concerned with specific economic units and with the way in which such units function.

Additional economic decisions facing each society are: How to **utilize** fully a nation's resources? How to **keep constant** the purchasing power of money and savings? Should production continue to **increase** or remain **stable**? The above decisions are studied in the context of **macroeconomics**, an area of the discipline concerned with the economy as a whole.

A. FILL IN THE BLANKS:

1. The basic problem facing people is that _____ needed for survival are _____.

2. In the face of scarcity, each society must decide: _____ to produce, _____ to produce it most efficiently, and ___ _____ it should be produced?

3. In different societies, these decisions are arrived at _____.

4. Some societies reach these decisions by relying on_____ and _____.

5. Other societies reach these decisions by the _____ of a ruler or ruling elite.

6. Still others use the _____ system dependent on_____ and _____, prices, profits, and losses.

7. The way in which these decisions are made are studied in the context of _____.

8. Societies must make additional _____ of an economic nature.

9. Societies must decide: how to _____ fully the nation's resources; how to keep the_____ _____of money and savings stable; and whether the economy should_____ or _____production.

10. These decisions are studied in the context of _____.

B. CHAPTER OVERVIEW

The goods and services that are produced in each society derive from the **resources** that exist naturally in that society, plus the **labor** of societal members. These natural resources are usually scarce and labor must be expended to accumulate them and utilize them. In economic terminology, resources are all those things that are **necessary for the production of goods and services**.

Thus, resources include **material things** (tools) and **human energy** (labor) used in producing goods and services.

Material things are either **natural** or **made by people**. The natural material things, called **land**, consist of land, minerals, and water. Material things made by people, called **capital**, consist of machinery, factories, shoes, pencils, etc. Together, labor, land, and capital are called **factors of production** because they are the basic elements that must be combined in the production of goods and services.

In addition to these basic factors, important elements in production are **technology, time, and efficiency**. Technology is the entire stock of **knowledge and skills** that a society possesses at any given time. **Time** is an economic resource that is scarce and precious. **Efficiency** is a way of obtaining the highest output of goods and services from a given combination of resources in the smallest amount of time. Resources are **versatile**: they can be put to different uses. But resources are also **finite**: they can be used up or destroyed, and cannot always be replaced. Resources and technology are the variables that affect the absolute **production possibilities** of society; but both resources and technology are fixed, so that production possibilities are ultimately **limited** (there is a limit to how much a society can produce).

Modern economies display such features as extreme **specialization** and division of labor, and they depend on **money** as the chief medium of exchange. Money is defined as a mechanism for facilitating barter. The **allocation** (distribution) of scarce resources is made differently in a market economy than in a command economy, although the two are just ideal models. Today, all economies are to some degree **mixed economies**, and the extent of the mixture and form that it takes are what determine whether an economic system is called **capitalistic, socialistic, or communistic**.

B. FILL IN THE BLANKS:

1. Resources include everything that is needed for_____ of goods and services.
2. Natural material things, called land, consist of _____, _____, and _____.
3. Material things made by people, called capital, consist of _____, _____, _____, etc.
4. The factors of production consist of _____, _____, and _____.
5. Additional elements of production are _____, _____, and _____.
6. Resources can be put to different uses: they are _____.
7. Resources can be used up or destroyed and cannot always be replaced: they are _____.
8. Both resources and technology are fixed, so that production is ultimately _____.
9. Some features of modern economies are: _____, division of _____, and _____as a medium of exchange.
10. Whether an economy is called capitalistic, socialistic, or communistic depends on the degree and form of_____ between a _____and a _____system.

C. CHAPTER OVERVIEW

Industrialization made necessary not only the physical changes in the **methods of production**, but also changes in **attitudes** and **values**. Before the Industrial Revolution, artisans worked at home and were paid for the raw material and labor. The profit motive was unknown. With industrialization, not only did the **profit motive** become preeminent, but work became specialized, **machinery** was used to speed it up, and workers and machinery were **housed in the same place** for greater efficiency. By now, the industrial system has long acquired specific patterns of organization. The chief characteristic of this system is the invention of a form of organization called the **corporation**.

The corporation is an enterprise **organized for large-scale production**. To raise money, owners of an enterprise sell shares of the company on the stock market. Buyers of the shares (shareholders) become co-owners of the new organization, or corporation. The corporation is **managed by executives** hired by a board of directors elected by the stockholders. This separation of ownership from management was designed to minimize the profit motive and maximize the welfare of the corporation. The corporation is a **legal entity** that can acquire resources, own assets, manufacture and sell goods, extend credit or incur debts, sue and be sued, and perform similar functions **distinct** from its owners. The shareholders lose only their investment in case of bankruptcy, but are **liable for nothing** else. But what has made the corporation by far the most effective form of business organization is its ability to **raise capital** by pooling the savings of thousands of investors.

There are problems with the corporation, too. First, many corporations have become **very large**, with practically a **monopoly of the market**, effectively squashing competition from smaller companies. This concentration of the productive wealth of the society in a few corporations is called **oligopoly**. Oligopoly is dangerous because lack of competition changes a free enterprise system into a monopoly; because financial power often translates into **political power**; because consumers are directed by **advertising** instead of competitive prices or quality; because of the **planned obsolescence** of products, ensuring ever greater consumption; and because of the **false needs** that are created only to supply consumers for the products. In addition, abuse occurs because many corporate executives and directors own controlling stock in the corporation; corporate directors of one company may be managers of another; and corporations own stock in other corporations.

New trends of corporations that lead to their ever greater size are **diversification and multinationalism**. Diversification is a corporation's acquisition of controlling shares in other corporations, often in totally different industries. Multinationalism is the habit of corporations to not merely export their products to foreign lands, but to **move** the production process into them, employing **cheaper local labor**.

C. FILL IN THE BLANKS:

1. Industrialization brought on physical changes in the_____
of production as well as changes in _____and
_____.

2. The industrial system was more efficient because it   brought
_____and _____under the same roof, giving employers
much more control.

3. The corporation is an enterprise organized for _____- _____
_____.

4. Shares of the corporation are sold on the _____ _____ and
shareholders become _____.

5. The corporation is managed by _____hired by
a_____ _____ _____voted in by the _____.

6. In a corporation, ownership is _____from management.

7. The corporation is a_____ _____capable of performing most
economic functions apart from its _____.

8. The corporation is an effective business organization because   of its ability to
_____investors' money.

9. One of the problems with the corporation is the concentration of corporate
power, or _____.

10. Some of the dangers in a concentration of productive power   include: lack
of _____, creating monopolies; financial power translating to
_____power, advertising directing   consumers instead
of_____ or _____, and the interrelationships of
_____.

D. CHAPTER OVERVIEW

For purposes of analysis the economy is divided into **three sectors**. The **primary sector** consists of the **extraction and processing of raw materials**, agriculture, fishing, mining, and forestry. The **secondary sector** is concerned with **manufacturing and building**, or turning raw materials into finished products. **The tertiary sector** represents the last stage of industrialization in which there is a great increase in **service** occupations.

With industrialization, there are dramatic **changes** in the sectors in which most workers are employed. In the early stages of industrialization (and before) the large majority of workers are employed in the primary sector. As industry progresses, the secondary sector shows a steady increase. The **tertiary sector** has had a tremendous spurt in growth from the beginning of the century, so that in this latest stage of industrialization the large **majority** of workers is employed in service occupations. This shift has resulted in important changes in the occupational structure because **more people** are becoming **professionals**, managers, or technicians, and there is **less need for unskilled or semiskilled occupations**. Such a transformation leads to changes in the stratification system of a society, causing chronic **unemployment** for that segment of the population that is unable to attain professionalization. **Professions** are not only specialized occupations, but occupations requiring **theoretical knowledge and training** in an art or a science. The attempts to professionalize have been successful among the white-collar workers of the tertiary sector, but not very successful in the first two sectors of the economy.

D. FILL IN THE BLANKS:

1. In order to study the economy, it is divided into _____.
2. Agriculture, mining, forestry, and extraction of raw materials belong in the_____ _____.
3. Manufacturing and building belong in the _____.
4. A large increase in service occupations occurs in the _____sector.
5. Industrialization brings about _____ _____in the_____ in which workers are employed.
6. In the early stages of industrialization, most workers are employed in the_____ sector.
7. In the latest stage of industrialization, most workers are employed in the_____ sector.
8. The occupational structure has undergone a shift as more people are becoming _____, _____, or _____.
9. There is less need for _____or _____workers.
10. Professions are _____occupations requiring _____knowledge and training.

E. CHAPTER OVERVIEW

Organization of labor in the United States began in 1880, when the AFL was reorganized and renamed and acquired a membership of four million of the five million unionized workers. The labor movement flourished again during the tenure of President **Roosevelt**, who **encouraged unionization** in the belief that it would give workers increased purchasing power, which in turn would **stimulate** the economy. The attempt to unionize **unskilled** workers resulted in the creation of the **CIO**, which merged with the AFL in 1955. The first unions were **horizontal,** or **craft** unions, in which workers were divided according to their skills. Later came the **industrial or vertical** unions, in which workers were organized according to the industry in which they worked. The most important contribution of the labor movement to the welfare of workers has been **collective bargaining.**

Today, organized labor is experiencing growth pains, partly as a result of the decline of the secondary sector and the growth of the tertiary sector, whose workers have traditionally avoided unionization, and partly because of other factors. **American labor** is engaged in a **battle** with foreign labor, just as the American economy is challenged by sharp **competition** from Japan and Western Europe. It may be necessary to take steps to restore some **self-discipline**, as well as invest in **educating** the work force to prepare it for the twenty-first century.

E. FILL IN THE BLANKS:

1. The American labor movement originated in the last two decades of the _____ century.
2. The labor movement began to flourish during the tenure of President

_____ .
3. President Franklin D. Roosevelt encouraged unionization because he thought it would give workers_____ _____ .
4. Horizontal unions are structured according to individual _____ .
5. Vertical unions include all workers employed in a specific _____ .
6. Organized labor is experiencing a decline in membership partly as a result of the growth of the _____ sector.
7. American labor is in competition with _____ labor, particularly that of _____ and_____ _____ .
8. American labor needs to be _____ and _____ .

TERMS TO REMEMBER

capital: All material objects made by humans. One of the factors of production.

capitalism: An economic system in which property belongs to private individuals; production is engaged in for a profit motive; and prices, wages, and profits are regulated by supply and demand, as well as competition. The welfare of the individual is the chief concern.

factors of production: Labor, land, capital, and entrepreneurship, or the basic elements that are combined in the production of goods and services.

finance capitalism: Capitalism associated with a later stage of industrialism in which business organizations are characterized by (1) dominance of investment banks and insurance companies, (2) large aggregates of capital, (3) ownership separate from management,   (4) appearance of the holding company, and (5) appearance of the corporation.

industrial capitalism: Capitalism associated with an early stage of industrialism in which business organizations were mainly concerned with manufacturing, mining, and transportation.

labor: Human resources. One of the factors of production.

land: Natural material things such as land, minerals, water. Another of the factors of production.

monopoly: A situation in which one firm produces the entire market supply of a specific product.

multinational corporations: Corporations that extend production to foreign nations at great profit to themselves (because labor is cheap and markets are expanded) but at the risk of being perceived as threats to the hosts.

oligopoly: A condition of high industrial concentration in which a small number of corporations dominate an entire industry, effectively preventing price competition.

opportunity cost: The sacrifice involved in making an economic choice.

production possibility limits: The optimum amount of production that a society can attain. Each society faces a production-possibility frontier beyond which it cannot produce.

resources: Everything that is needed for the production of goods and services.

HOW MUCH DO YOU RECALL? TEST YOUR KNOWLEDGE

MULTIPLE CHOICE QUESTIONS

1. The primary function of the economy as a social institution is to:
    a. guarantee prosperity for all
    b. provide a blueprint showing people how to survive
    c. produce surpluses in all goods and services
    d. none of the above

2. Each society must make the following decisions of an economic nature regarding the:

a. time, place, and quantity of production
b. assessment, collection, and counting of taxes
c. measurement of land, water, and minerals
d. production, distribution, and consumption of goods and services

3. Resources are defined as:
a. anything that is made by people
b. anything that is produced in factories
c. anything that is derived from natural ingredients
d. everything that is needed for the production of goods and services including human energy

4. Land, labor, capital, and entrepreneurship are called:
a. raw materials
b. impetus to upward mobility
c. factors of production
d. external devices

5. A society's economic system is largely determined by its concept of:
a. profit
b. property
c. surplus
d. production

6. The following factors are important in production:
a. technology
b. time
c. efficiency
d. all of the above

7. The foremost advantage of a corporation is its:
a. ability to accumulate vast amounts of capital in a short time
b. capacity for protracted periods of employment
c. ability to profit from the labor of its employees
d. necessity to exhibit the latest technology

8. Professionalization means:
a. excessive upward mobility
b. interlocking directorates
c. racial polarization
d. none of the above

9. The economy, in relation to resources, deals with their:
a. production

b. distribution
c. consumption
d. none of the above
e. all of the above

10. Which economic orientations govern Western industrial societies?
a. Tradition
b. Command
c. Free Market
d. both market and command

11. The production possibilities frontier refers to:
a. the amount of each commodity that can be produced given available resources
b. unlimited production of one commodity
c. limitless output of commodities
d. the fact that Third World nations do not allow their commodities to cross the borders into industrial societies.

12. When a few powerful corporations dominate an industry, the condition is called:
a. a free market for all
b. monopoly
c. oligopoly
d. government control

13. When Nabisco buys Domino Pizza, the process is called:
a. raiding
b. planned obsolescence
c. multinationalism
d. diversification

14. Unions today face some of the following problems:
a. the effects of the iron law of oligarchy
b. decline of heavy industry
c. loss of membership
d. all of the above
e. none of the above

15. Factors in the development of capitalism included:
a. the entrepreneurial spirit
b. wage labor
c. ownership of the factors of production
d. all of the above

ANSWERS TO FILL IN THE BLANKS:

A.
1. resources, scarce
2. what, how, for whom
3. differently
4. custom and tradition
5. command
6. market, supply and demand
7. microeconomics
8. decisions
9. utilize, purchasing power, increase, stabilize
10. macroeconomics

B.
1. production
2. land, minerals, water
3. machinery, factories, objects
4. labor, land, capital
5. technology, time, and efficiency
6. versatile
7. finite
8. limited
9. specialization, labor, money
10. mixture, command, market

C.
1. method, attitudes, values
2. workers, machinery
3. large-scale production
4. stock market, co-owners
5. executives, board of directors, stockholders
6. separate
7. legal entity, owners
8. pool
9. oligopoly
10. competition, political, need, quality, management

D.
1. three sectors
2. primary sector
3. secondary sector
4. tertiary sector
5. dramatic changes, sectors
6. primary
7. tertiary

8. professionals, managers, technicians
9. unskilled, semiskilled
10. specialized, theoretical

E. 1. nineteenth
2. Roosevelt
3. increased purchasing power
4. skills
5. industry
6. tertiary
7. foreign, Japan, Western Europe
8. reeducated, disciplined

ANSWERS TO MULTIPLE CHOICE QUESTIONS:

1. b
2. d
3. d
4. c
5. b
6. d
7. a
8. d
9. e
10. d
11. a
12. c
13. d
14. d
15. d

CHAPTER 18: PRINCIPLES OF ECONOMIC BEHAVIOR

MICROECONOMICS AND MACROECONOMICS

In this chapter, you will learn:

1. the difference between microeconomics and macroeconomics;
2. who the participants are in the market system;
3. what is the essence of the price system;
4. what are the market forces;
5. the need for a public sector and for government intervention in the economy;
6. about the economic goals of the society;
7. the instruments at the government's disposal for intervening in the economy and the reason for their imperfect functioning;
8. the major economic problems faced by the economy, and how the American economy responds to them.

TOPICAL OUTLINE

I. THE SMALL PICTURE AND THE LARGE PICTURE
    A. Market Mechanisms
    B. Who Makes Decisions?
    C. Who Participates in the Economy?
    D. Markets
    E. Circular Flow

II. MARKET FORCES
    A. Demand, Supply, and Price
        1. Equilibrium
    B. The Principle of Laissez-Faire and Public Needs

III. A MACROVIEW
    A. The Public Interest: Socioeconomic Goals
        1. Full Employment
        2. Desirable Mix of Output
        3. High and Equitably Distributed Incomes
        4. Reasonable Price Stability
        5. Adequate Growth

IV. INSTRUMENTS OF PUBLIC POLICY
    A. Fiscal Policy
    B. The Function of Price and Employment Stabilizers
        1. Federal Budget

2. Fiscal Decision Making

V. MONETARY POLICY
   A. Banks
   B. Interest Rates
   C. Regulating Banks
   D. The Federal Reserve or the FED

VI.   INCOMES POLICY
   A. Phillips Curve
   B. Full Employment Inflation Tradeoff

VII.   ECONOMIC PROBLEMS AND GOVERNMENT RESPONSE
   A. Depression or Severe Recession
   B: Excessive Demand and Inflation
   C. Inflation and Unemployment
   D. Business Cycles
      1. Demand-Side Theories
      2. Supply-Side Theories
      3. Eclectic Theories
      4. Theory and Reality
      5. Fitting Into The Global Economy

A. CHAPTER OVERVIEW

The **American** economy is a **mixed market economy** in which most workers are employed in the tertiary sector. In a market economy, decisions as to what is produced are basically made by **consumers** through a **price system**, meaning that the more consumers are willing to spend for a certain product, the more producers are willing to manufacture it. The participants in a market economy include: **households**, or those who live under one roof and make financial decisions as a unit; **firms**, or units that decide how to use labor, land, and capital (the factors of production) and which goods and services to produce; and **central authorities**, which are all public agencies, **government** bodies, and other organizations under the control of various levels of government.

In economic terminology, **markets** are **abstractions** referring to the demand for, the supply, and the price of a given product on a local or global level. **Product markets** are those in which firms sell their products; **factor or resource markets** are those in which households sell those factors of production which they control.

The **circular flow** is the process in which households earn money by selling their labor to firms, and firms, with that labor, produce goods and services which they sell to householders who pay for them with money earned with their labor. (Circular flow--from product markets to factor markets and back again.) The circular flow is **not** entirely a **closed** system because of withdrawals and injections. **Withdrawals** is income received by households that is not returned to firms, or income received by firms that is not returned to households. **Injections** is income received by firms that does not originate from the spending of households, and income received by households that does not originate from the spending of firms.

A. FILL IN THE BLANKS:

1. In a market economy, decisions as to what to produce are made   by _____through a _____system.
2. Participants in a market economy include: _____, _____, and_____ _____.
3. Markets are _____representing _____, _____, and _____on a local or global level.
4. Firms sell their products in _____markets; households sell their factors of production in _____or_____ markets.
5. Circular flow is the process in which factors of production flow from_____ _____to _____ _____and back again.
6. The circular flow is interrupted by _____and _____.

B. CHAPTER OVERVIEW

Market forces through which participants try to **maximize** their happiness, profits, or the general welfare are **demand, supply, and price**. Two basic exchanges take place in the market: energy and labor flow in one direction, and money flows in the opposite direction. **Supply** is what an individual gives up in an exchange. **Demand** is what an individual obtains. Each participant in the market is at some time both on the supply and on the demand side. Demand is expressed as the individual's willingness and ability to buy a specific number of products at a specific price. This is graphically illustrated by a demand curve. Supply represents the combined willingness of individuals or firms to supply specific resources or products at specific prices; this is expressed by the supply curve. The point at which supply and demand curves **intersect**, meaning that the quantity supplied equals the price buyers are willing to pay, is called **equilibrium**. Increasing or decreasing purchases according to changes in price is called **price elasticity**; demand is elastic when people buy more of a good in response to a change in price; and inelastic when they buy little even when the price is drastically cut.

The content and flow of goods and services, as well as prices at which they are exchanged, are determined by the independent actions of individual buyers and sellers without the intervention of any central authority. This is called the **"laissez-faire"** doctrine, or leaving things alone. The advantages of such a system include: it allows people to feel free from constraint, to maximize each participant's goal, to use society's scarce resources in the production of those goods and services for which there is greatest demand, and to distribute goods and services on the basis of the amount of purchasing power of each participant. Thus, the market system answers **automatically** the three basic questions faced by every economy. The disadvantages of the market system include the fact that no provision is made for **public goods**; and it works to the advantage of those who already possess some resources, thus **perpetuating inequality**. Those in control over a significant proportion of productive resources are able to change market outcomes in their own interest.

B. FILL IN THE BLANKS

1. Market forces that maximize participants' happiness, profits, or general welfare include _____, _____, and _____.
2. The two basic exchanges that take place in the market are:
_____and _____flow in one direction, and _____flows in the opposite direction.
3. Demand is what an individual _____in an exchange; supply is what the individual _____ _____in an exchange.
4. One advantage of the market system is that it answers _____the three questions faced by every society.

C. CHAPTER OVERVIEW

Because some of the results of the market system are not **consonant** with the goals of the society, market economies have had to accept a degree of **government intervention** in spite of the laissez-faire doctrine. Although not easily defined, most would agree that societal goals include: **full employment** (between 4 and 5 percent unemployment); a desirable **mix of output**; high and **equitably distributed incomes**; reasonable **price stability**; **adequate growth**--to produce enough goods and services for the greatest number of people. Public policy is used to achieve some of these goals: taxes and subsidies are used to redistribute unequal purchasing power; where there is no demand for a good or service, yet there is a need for it; to counteract negative effects of the economy, such as congestion, pollution, urban decay, etc; controlling inflation; making sure that economic growth keeps up with population growth; and ensuring that investments are stimulated enough to increase productivity.

The government uses **fiscal actions**, **monetary** actions, and direct **regulation** to intervene in the economy. Fiscal policy is the use of **public expenditures** and **taxation powers** to change the outcomes of the economy. Taxes result in transferring buying power from the private to the public sector. By spending or not spending tax revenues, the government **affects** the level and mix of output, **redistributes** incomes, affects price stability and growth. **Fiscal** policy is known for its function as a **stabilizer**; it is a tool for achieving full employment and stable prices. When the government spends money, it **expands demand**, bringing full employment, resulting in higher consumption, further spurring demand, a process called the **multiplier effect**. **Inflation**, or excessive demand, is curbed by government action too: the government reduces its spending and raises taxes. As a result of its need to intervene in the economy, the Federal Budget is often out of balance, the government engaging in **deficit** spending an accumulating a huge public debt.

Monetary policy refers to the use of money and credit controls to affect economic outcomes. **Banks**, by extending or limiting credit, affect the money supply. By **raising or lowering interest rates**, banks can **stimulate** greater or lesser borrowing, affecting the amount of purchasing power in the circular flow. The ability of banks to extend credit is limited by the need to have the proper **reserve ratio**--the proportion of deposits that must be retained for withdrawal, transfer, and government regulation. The **Federal Reserve Bank** is the principal regulator of the money supply; it can establish minimum reserve requirements; it charges interest to lend to member banks; it can buy and sell government securities, increasing or decreasing the amount of money in circulation. .

C. FILL IN THE BLANKS:

1. Some of the goals our society aims for are:_____ _____,
a desirable_____ __ _____, high and equal _____,
reasonable_____ _____, and adequate _____.
2. Some of these goals are achieved through_____
such as _____and subsidies.
3. The government intervenes in the economy through _____
actions, _____ actions, and _____ regulation.
4. Fiscal policy is the use of _____and
_____powers to affect the outcomes of the economy.
5. Taxes transfer _____ _____from the _____to   the
_____ sector.
6. By spending or failing to spend tax revenues, the government _____the
mix and level of output ,_____incomes, affects price and _____.
7. Fiscal policy is known in its function of _____.
8. Monetary policy refers to the use of _____and
_____controls to affect the outcomes of the economy.

216

TERMS TO REMEMBER

budget surplus: A surplus that occurs when the government's revenues are greater than its expenditures.

central authorities: All public agencies, generally referred to as "the government."

circular flow: Movement from product markets to resource markets and back again, which is interrupted by withdrawals and injections.

deficit spending: Spending that occurs when the government's expenditures are greater than its revenues.

discount rate: The interest rate charged by the Federal Reserve Bank for lending money to member banks.

discretionary spending: The portion of the federal budget that consists of current spending, rather than carryovers from previous years.

disposable income: National income less taxes and plus welfare payments. What people really have to spend or to save

equilibrium: The price and quantity at which both buyers and sellers are compatible--the quantity supplied equals the price buyers are willing to pay.

factor or resource markets: Markets in which households sell the factors of production that they control.

firms: Units that decide how to use labor, land, and capital and which goods and services to produce.

fiscal policy: The use of public expenditures and taxation powers by the government to change the outcomes of the economy.

full employment: A low rate of unemployment, between 4 and 5 percent.

GNP per capita: The total output of the economy divided by the total population.

Gross Domestic Product (GDP): The market value of all goods and services produced every year within the borders of a nation by residents and nonresidents alike.

Gross National Product (GNP): The total value in dollar-units of all goods and services produced in a nation during a given year.

household: All the people who live under one roof and who make financial decisions as a unit. Also called the
consumer.

marginal productivity: The value people's work adds to total output.

market demand: The combined willingness of individuals and firms to buy a specific number of products at a specific price.

market supply: The combined willingness of individuals or firms to supply specific resources or products at specific prices.

monetary policy: The use of money and credit to control economic outcomes.

multiplier effect: Government spending that produces more income, results in higher consumption expenditures, and translates into a higher aggregate demand.

Net National Product (NNP): GNP less cost of depreciation for tools and machinery.

Phillips curve: A graphic illustration of the conflict between full employment and price stability: lower rates of unemployment are usually accompanied by higher rates of inflation.

product markets: Markets in which firms sell their production of goods and services.

uncontrollable expenditures: Expenditures from previous years built into the annual federal budget.

HOW MUCH DO YOU RECALL? TEST YOUR KNOWLEDGE

MULTIPLE CHOICE QUESTIONS

1. In a market economy, decisions about production are made by:
    a. command of ruling elite
    b. traditional forces in society
    c. a price system
    d. competing elites

2. Which of the following groups are involved in market transactions:
    a. Households, firms, and central authorities
    b. consumers, producers, distributors
    c. wholesalers, shippers, workers
    d. advertisers, customers, retailers

3. A circular flow occurs from:
    a. demand to supply
    b. supply to demand
    c. banks to consumers
    d. product markets to factor markets and back

4. In a market economy, who gets the goods and services produced by firms?
    a. All members of society equally
    b. Only individuals involved in producing them
    c. Consumers who have the desire for them and the money to pay for them
    d. The strongest and smartest individuals in society

5. What are the goals of the participants in the mixed American economy?
    a. Consumers try to maximize their happiness
    b. Firms try to maximize their profits
    c. Government tries to maximize the general welfare
    d. All of the above

6. The two basic exchanges that take place in an economy are:
    a. energy and labor in one direction, and money in the other
    b. supply and demand
    c. wholesale and retail
    d. profit and deficit
    e. both a and b

7. When demand is inelastic prices:
    a. go down
    b. go up
    c. stay the same
    d. equal costs

8. Demand is defined as:
    a. the circular manner in which market transactions occur
    b. an individual's willingness and ability to buy a specific product at a specific price

c. what firms are willing and able to supply
d. what government allows consumers to buy

9. Full employment really means:
    a. zero percent unemployment
    b. twenty to twenty-five percent unemployment
    c. four to five percent unemployment
    d. that all able-bodied persons can find work

10. An insufficient demand for, and an oversupply of, goods and services leads to falling prices and a condition known as:
    a. inflation
    b. deflation
    c. circular flow
    d. price elasticity of demand

11. An insufficient supply of goods and services and inability of demand to catch up leads to rising prices and a condition known as:
    a. inflation
    b. deflation
    c. supply and demand
    d. marginal productivity

12. When increased income results in greater spending and consequently a higher aggregate demand, the condition is called the:
    a. rippling effect
    b. Phillips curve
    c. multiplier effect
    d. inflationary spiral

13. The principal role of the Federal Reserve Bank is:
    a. chief regulator of the money supply
    b. to insure depositors against loss of deposits
    c. to lend money to individuals
    d. to borrow money from the federal government

14. When cars are offered at low prices but people still do not   buy them, the situation is one in which:
    a. demand is elastic
    b. demand is inelastic
    c. there is aggregate demand
    d. exchange takes place

15. Some of the advantages of a market economy include:
    a. all participants get some satisfaction

    b. scarce resources are put into goods that are in demand
    c. economic output is available to those who can pay the price
    d. none of the above
  e. all of the above

16.   When supply and demand are essentially equal, the economy is said to be in:
    a. a recession
    b. equilibrium
    c. equivalence
    d. abeyance

17.   During depressions or severe recessions, the government:
    a. increases expenditures
    b. cuts taxes
    c. prints paper money
    d. only a and b (cuts taxes and increases expenditures)

18.   Market mechanisms:
    a. work to the advantage of those with existing resources
    b. advance social equality
    c. serve the interests of the majority
    d. provide for the production of public goods

19.   A problem with laissez-faire economic policy is that there is:
    a. no flexibility
    b. no provision for public goods
    c. no profit motive
    d. responsiveness to demand

20.   Adam Smith would approve of governmental support of:
    a. full employment
    b. protection of environment
    c. care for sick and needy
    d. none of the above
    e. all of the above

21.   The problems encountered by the public sector include:
    a. difficulty in dismissing employees for incompetence
    b. small size of government agencies
    c. low expenditures
    d. none of the above
    e. all of the above

22. Inflation results when:

a. demand exceeds supply
b. supply exceeds demand
c. there is control of purchasing power
d. consumers have no purchasing power

23. The problem that arises when the government participates in the economy is that it:
a. contributes to the training of skilled workers
b. contributes to research and technology
c. borrows large sums of money
d. takes profits away from firms

24. The government can curb excessive aggregate demand (inflation) by:
a. decreasing taxes on consumers
b. increasing spending
c. decreasing taxes on firms
d. none of the above
e. all of the above

25. When the government must pay for warships based on commitments made five years previously, the spending is called:
a. discretionary
b. uncontrollable
c. balanced
d. unavoidable

26. In order to deal with a situation of inflation and unemployment, the government must use:
a. incomes policy
b. antitrust action
c. regular monetary and fiscal policies
d. none of the above
e. all of the above

27. The government's efforts at helping solve economic problems are hindered by difficulties in:
a. measurement
b. interpretation
c. implementation
d. none of the above
e. all of the above

28. If the GNP increases by 8% and prices increase by 3%, the actual growth rate is:
   a. 11%
   b. 5%
   c. 8%
   d. 3%

29. In recent years, the income of the wealthy and affluent:
   a. remained unchanged
   b. decreased
   c. increased
   d. was redistributed to equalize the standard of living

30. In deciding to spend or not to spend tax revenues, the government:
   a. affects the level and mix of output
   b. redistributes incomes
   c. affects price stability and growth
   d. all of the above
   e. none of the above

31. Governmental action is used to solve all but which one of the following problems?
   a. Lack of competition in the public sector
   b. Depression or recession
   c. Excessive demand and inflation
   d. Unemployment and inflation

32. The American economy:
   a. has shown a great increase in the tertiary sector
   b. has shown an increase in professionalism
   c. has failed to protect consumers from greedy producers
   d. all of the above
   e. none of the above

ANSWERS TO FILL IN THE BLANKS:

A.   1. consumers, price
     2. households, firms, central authorities
     3. abstractions, demand, supply, price
     4. product, factor, resource
     5. product markets, factor markets
     6. withdrawals, injections

B.　　1. demand, supply, price
　　　　2. energy, labor, money
　　　　3. obtains, gives up
　　　　4. automatically

C.　　1. full employment, mix of output, incomes, price stability, growth
　　　　2. policy, taxes
　　　　3. fiscal, monetary, direct
　　　　4. public expenditures, taxation
　　　　5. buying power, private, public
　　　　6. affects, redistributes, and growth
　　　　7. stabilizer
　　　　8. money, credit

ANSWERS TO MULTIPLE CHOICE QUESTIONS:

1. c
2. a
3. d
4. c
5. d
6. e
7. a
8. b
9. c
10. b
11. a
12. c
13. a
14. b
15. e
16. b
17. d
18. a
19. b
20. d
21. a
22. a
23. c
24. d
25. b
26. e

27. e
28. b
29. c
30. d
31. a
32. d

CHAPTER 19: NATION AMONG NATIONS:
PERSPECTIVES ON INTERNATIONAL RELATIONS

In this chapter, you will learn

1. the definition of international relations;
2. theoretical perspectives from which scholars examine the international system;
3. who are the participants in the international political system;
4. the objectives of states, as evidenced by foreign policy and its instruments;
5. that states also attain objectives by means of diplomacy;
6. the importance of the concept of power; and how the of "balance of power" has changed;
7. what is the role of the United Nations.

TOPICAL OUTLINE

I. REGIONS OF THE WORLD
   A. Europe
   B. The Former Soviet Union
   C. The Middle East
   D. Asia
   E. Pacific Rim
   F. Sub-Saharan Africa
   G. Latin America
   H. Anglo America
      1. Other Ways of Classifying States
         a. First, Second, Third World nations
         b. Rich Nations and Poor Nations

II. THEORETICAL PERSPECTIVES ON INTERNATIONAL RELATIONS
   A. Realism

III. CONTEMPORARY PERSPECTIVES
   A Pluralism
   B Globalism
   C Neorealism

IV. PARTICIPANTS IN THE INTERNATIONAL SYSTEM
   A. Actors

V. THE STATE AND THE NATION
   A. Classification of States
      1. Nonstate Actors

VI. THE GOALS OF STATES
  A. The Competition of Objectives

VII. MEANS OF ACHIEVING GOALS: FOREIGN POLICY
  A. The Purpose of Foreign Policy
  B. Types of Foreign-Policy Decisions

VIII. AMERICAN FOREIGN POLICY
  A. Goals
  B. The Role of Ideology
  C. Instruments of Foreign Policy
    1. The United Nations
    2. Foreign Aid
    3. Collective Security
    4. The Military

IX. PROPAGANDA

X. DIPLOMACY AND DIPLOMATS
  A. Treaties and Alliances
  B. Morality in Foreign Policy
  C. Power

XI. THE BALANCE-OF-POWER SYSTEM
  A. The Multipolar System
  B. The World Wars
  C. A New Multipolar World

A. Chapter Overview

The discipline of international relations is a vast and complex field. It concerns activities as diverse as war and humanitarian assistance, trade and investment, tourism and the Olympic Games. The core of inquiry of this discipline consists of three questions: (1) How do states **act,** and particularly why do they act the way they do toward one another (what is their national interest as expressed by their foreign policies)? (2) How do states **attain their goals** and objectives (what are their capabilities in terms of power)? (3) What are the main characteristics of the **interaction** between states (diplomacy, aid, exchange, cooperation)?

The geographic location and resources at the disposal of states affect their role on the world stage. **Europe** consists of 38 countries with a total population of one-half billion people. The countries are politically, economically, and even culturally similar, though differences in languages and religion remain. The region exhibits the most advanced form of regional cooperation in a variety of economic and security organizations, such as the European Union (EU) and the

North Atlantic Treaty Organization (NATO). Such cooperation is needed since Europe historically had been the site of numerous wars. Although no longer the dominant power in the world, Europe is competing successfully on the world stage in economic and technological matters, and offers its citizens a high quality of life as measured by wealth, life expectancy, and education.

The Former Soviet Union is no longer monolithic because of the breakup of the Soviet Union in 1991. This breakup caused the fifteen republics that made it up to become independent countries. Russia is the largest of these, but is currently in a critical situation economically and politically. Used to being a nuclear world power, Russia, which straddles Europe and Asia, has had difficulty adapting to democracy and capitalism after seventy years of communism. The rest of the former Soviet Union consists of Slavic nations such as Ukraine and Belarus, Asian nations such as Armenia, Georgia, and Azerbaijan, and   five Islamic countries, of which the largest is Uzbekistan.

The Middle East consists of desert and semiarid grassland and is located at a point where northern Africa, southwest Asia, and southern Europe come together. It is a resource-poor area, except for a dramatic exception: some of the countries are rich in oil, the earth's most lucrative commodity. The unifying factor in the region is Islam.

Asia has seen a phenomenal growth in the last several years. Japan and the smaller nations of Taiwan, South Korea, Singapore, Malaysia, and Hong Kong exhibited until recently one of the world's highest GDPs per capita. Their economies were export-driven and managed, and seemed invincible. Of late, there has been a retrenchment, which may or may not be overcome in the near future. The three most important countries in the region are Japan, India, and China, the last two with populations hovering around one billion.

Sub-Saharan Africa is geographically the largest of the world's regions, containing 44 nations, most of which were created by colonial powers and most of which have gained their independence only since the 1960s.The job of building nations out of the disparate tribes speaking hundreds of languages has been very difficult. The area is plagued by the highest incidence of poverty, a short life expectancy and some of the lowest living standards in the world.

Anglo America refers to the continent of North America, containing the United States and Canada. It is the wealthiest and politically most powerful region in the world. Enjoying many natural resources, fertile soils, a large population (more than 260 million for the United States, only 30 million for Canada), and political stability, the region exhibits one of the highest standards of living and high life expectancy. Its culture appears to be a role model for the rest of the world.

Latin America includes the countries of Central America as well as the whole continent of South America. It is a very large area whose unifying motifs are the Spanish language and culture (with the exception of Brazil, which is Portuguese-speaking) and the Roman Catholic religion. The region has been plagued by political instability and has attained a degree of democratization only in the recent past. Severe economic problems remain and a deep gap exists between rich and poor.

A. FILL IN THE BLANKS

1. The core of the discipline of international relations revolves around a. how states _____, b. how states _____ ___ _____, and c. how states _____.

2. There are _____ countries in Europe, with a total population of __ ___ ___people.

3. Although there are differences in language and religion, these countries are essentially_____ in political stability, economics, etc.

4. Europe displays much _____ _____ because of its history.

5. The former Soviet Union is today made up of _____republics, of which the largest is _____.

6. Used to being a nuclear _____ _____, Russia has had difficulty adjusting to _____ and _____.

7. In addition to Russia, the former Soviet Union consists of _____, _____, and _____ nations.

8. The most precious commodity in the Middle East is _____.

9. The unifying factor in the Middle East region is_____

10. The three most important nations in Asia are _____, _____, and _____.

11. Japan and the smaller nations of _____, _____, and ____ ___ have seen a dramatic economic growth in the last decade.

12. The two nations whose populations hover around one billion each are _____ and _____.

13. Geographically the largest of the world's regions with 44 countries is ___ _____.

14. This area is also the _____, with short ___ _____and ____standard of living.

15. The wealthiest and most powerful region of the world is _____ _____ which consists of _____ and _____.

16. This area exhibits the highest standard of living due to its many _____, its large _____, and its political _____.

17. The countries of Central and South America make up the region referred to as _____ _____.

18. The unifying elements of this region are the _____language and culture, and the _____ _____religion.

19. The region has achieved a degree of _____ only in the recent past.

229

20. There are great gaps between the _____and the _____ in this region, which leads to political _____.

B. CHAPTER OVERVIEW

Interaction between and among states is the basic definition of **international relations**, a subdiscipline of political science. The discipline is analyzed from a variety of **theoretical** and **dimensional** levels which result in a multiplicity of conclusions. Most scholars agree that the most important participants in the international system are **states**, that states attempt to attain specific **objectives** by means of **foreign policies** and **diplomacy**, and that underlying the international system is **power** understood as **military strength**. Power in this context is defined as the capacity of a nation to use its tangible and intangible resources in such a way as to affect the behavior of other nations. The power of a nation is not always dependent on its capabilities. **National power** is influenced by both **psychological** and **relational factors**--how others view a nation and how powerful one nation is in relation to others.

Foreign policy is intended to **protect** and promote **national independence**, honor, **security**, and well-being. It is designed to pursue **national interest** as it is defined by each nation. Some political commentators believe that the pursuit of power is the central concern of national interest. Others suggest that national interest is determined by both **power and morality**. The goals that nations seek may be divided into those that are **competitive or absolute**, those that are **clearly** defined or diffuse, those that are **declaratory** or **action-oriented**, and those that are **static** or **dynamic**. The nature of national interest is not explained by single-factor concepts.

B. FILL IN THE BLANKS:

1. Interaction between and among states is the basic definition of

_____ _____.

2. The discipline is analyzed from a number of theoretical and   dimensional levels resulting in a multiplicity of _____.

3. Underlying the international system is _____ understood as _____ _____.

4. In this context, power is defined as the _____ of a nation to use its tangible and intangible resources in such a way as to _____the behavior of other nations.

5. Foreign policy is intended to protect and promote national

_____, _____, and _____-_____.   6. The goals that nations seek include those that are _____ or _____, clearly defined or _____, declaratory or _____, static or _____.

C. CHAPTER OVERVIEW

Foreign policy is made by **individuals** who are pressured and influenced by others, by psychological factors, and by specific conditions and are limited by the organizational context in which they operate. There are **three types** of foreign policy decisions: (1) **general** foreign-policy decisions, expressed in policy statements and direct actions; (2) **administrative** decisions made by the governmental bureaucracy; and (3) **crisis** decisions made when one state feels that a specific situation marks a turning point in its relationships with one or more other states.

Foreign policy is affected by domestic policy. American domestic policy is guided by the **democratic ideology**, including revolutionary ideals and the concept of freedom. Although Americans do not always act according to this ideology, they are officially committed to it. The problematic aspect of foreign policy is that other nations subscribe to other ideologies, some of which **conflict** with the American ideology.

In the course of American foreign policy, the country has been **isolationist, interventionist, internationalist**, and a supporter of the **containment** policy, or rabidly anticommunist. This last policy led the United States into the unpopular and costly Vietnam War. In the 1970s, American foreign policy was characterized by the spirit of **detente**.

C. FILL IN THE BLANKS

1. Foreign policy is made by _____, _____
_____, and _____ _____.
2. Foreign policy decisions may be _____,_____, and

_____.
3. American domestic policy is guided by the_____

_____.
4. In the course of American foreign policy, the nation has been
_____, _____, and a supporter of
the containment policy.

D. CHAPTER OVERVIEW.

The analysis of foreign policy should include questions regarding nation's **values, roles, and instruments**. The values of American foreign policy changed from a **defense of democracy** to rabid **anticommunism**, and are in the process of changing toward peaceful **coexistence**. The instruments of foreign policy, or tools with which something is accomplished in the international arena by manipulating nations, include: the **United Nations**, foreign **aid**, **collective security, the military establishment**, and **propaganda**.

The United Nations is not powerful enough because most decisions that affect world peace are made by the governments of the major powers. American aid to nations around the world has probably helped contain communism and has also helped the economies of various nations. **Treaties and security arrangements** improve relations between and among nations, but they are never really totally dependable.

Although the United States professes to want to **halt** the production of arms, weapons production and stockpiling continue to **escalate**, although there are some signs that the arms race is abating. The arms race spirals because each power must keep up with the technology of other powers if possession of nuclear arms is to act as a deterrent to mutual destruction. Propaganda--an ideology that someone tries to spread to convince others of its rightness--sometimes leads us to stretch the truth or to direct it at our own citizens. Many government agencies and departments are engaged in propaganda.

D. FILL IN THE BLANKS:

1. Foreign-policy analysis includes _____,
_____, and _____.
2. Instruments of foreign policy are the_____ _____,
_____ ____, _____ _____, the military, and
propaganda.
3. The United Nations is not powerful enough because most decisions are made by the _____of the major powers.
4. Treaties and security arrangements are never really   totally
_____.
5. Propaganda sometimes leads us to_____the truth.

E. CHAPTER OVERVIEW

Morality has always been considered a necessity in foreign policy, at least on the part of the "civilized" world. But it is **difficult to define** morality, which is relative to time and circumstances. It appears that for now it is necessary to settle for morality in the form of rhetoric rather than as a prescription for actual behavior.

Diplomacy is the conduct of international relations by **negotiation**. Its purpose is the pursuit of national goals without offending any nation. Diplomacy is an old procedure, although it has changed in character in this century. The power of diplomacy is **limited** because there are fundamental differences among the major powers and because diplomats in democratic countries are unsure of their roles.

A **balance of power** was maintained for several hundred years after the creation of nation-states by a **system of shifting alliances** that ensured that **no single state** or coalition would become **stronger** than any other. This **multipolar** balance of power began to decline at the turn of the century, and following World War II a bipolar system--with the United States and the Soviet Union as its poles--took its place. Today, the balance of power is again shifting, but it is not clear in what direction.

E. FILL IN THE BLANKS

1. Morality is _____ to time and circumstances.
2. The conduct of international relations by negotiation is the definition of
_____.
3. The power of diplomacy is _____ because there are fundamental _____ among the major powers.
4. A balance of power was maintained for several centuries by a system of
_____ _____.
5. The balance of power ensured that no single state or coalition would
_____ _____ than the others.
6. The _____ balance of power began to decline at the turn of the century, and a _____ system took its place.

TERMS TO REMEMBER

administrative foreign policy: Decisions made by the government bureaucracy.

containment: American foreign policy in the period following World War II, attempting to contain what were perceived as the imperialist goals of the Soviet Union.

crisis foreign policy: Urgent decisions made when one state feels that a situation will mark a turning point in its relationship with another state. Crisis decisions are a combination of general and administrative decisions.

detente: Foreign policy dependent on peaceful negotiations rather than containment.

diplomacy: The conduct of international relations by negotiation.

foreign policy: Goals intended to protect and promote national independence, national honor, national security, and national well being.

general foreign policy: Decisions expressed in policy statements and direct actions.

internationalism: American foreign policy in the late 1930s and during World War II, in which there was a commitment to principles of nonaggression and self-determination.

interventionism: American foreign policy of the early twentieth century, in which the United States intervened militarily in other nation-states to "make the world safe for democracy."

isolationism: Early American foreign policy of staying clear of permanent or entangling relationships and alliances with other nation states.

Truman doctrine: Foreign policy giving the support of the United States to free nations so that they could maintain their free institutions and national integrity against the imposition of totalitarian regimes.

HOW MUCH DO YOU RECALL? TEST YOUR KNOWLEDGE

MULTIPLE CHOICE QUESTIONS

1. "The capacity of a nation to use its resources to affect the behavior of other nations" is a definition of:
   a. foreign policy
   b. diplomacy
   c. power in the context of international relations
   d. international law

2. Foreign policy decisions may be categorized into those that are:
   a. general
   b. administrative
   c. crisis
   d. all of the above
   e. none of the above

3. Among the goals of United States foreign policy are the protection of:
   a. the nation's physical security
   b. the security of our main allies
   c. the economic security of the nation
   d. all of the above
   e. none of the above

4. The oldest goal of American foreign policy, articulated by the Monroe Doctrine, was to:
   a. develop friendly ties with the Soviet Union

b. keep peace in the Middle East
c. keep foreign powers out of North and South America
d. be the first atomic power

5. Realism posits that:
    a. the state is a rational actor in international relations
    b. economics and culture are central to politics
    c. foreign policy is often self-contradictory
    d. the essence of politics is the pursuit of wealth

6. "Gunboat Diplomacy" was used in which stage of American foreign policy?
    a. Isolationism
    b. Containment
    c. Interventionism
    d. The Cold War

7. The term "detente" has been used to denote a kind of foreign policy based on:
    a. aggressiveness
    b. containment
    c. peaceful negotiations
    d. hiding behind an iron curtain

8. What should an analysis of foreign policy include?
    a. Values
    b. Roles
    c. Instruments
    d. All of the above
    e. None of the above

9. The view that the U.S. ought to remain involved in the international community by means of providing foreign aid, arms control, and U.N. peacekeeping efforts is called:
    a. isolationism
    b. cooperative internationalism
    c. interventionism
    d. laissez-faire containment

10. The military-industrial complex depends on:
    a. huge defense spending
    b. a large bureaucracy
    c. research in military technology
    d. all of the above
    e. none of the above

11. American propaganda:
    a. delivers America's message to the world
    b. involves several government agencies
    c. sometimes distorts the truth
    d. none of the above
    e. all of the above

12. Diplomacy today gives diplomats:
    a. great discretion in making policy decisions
    b. limited roles as messengers
    c. charge of summit conferences
    d. starring roles as celebrities

13. Neorealism maintains that states face three problems:
    a. other states, elites, and classes
    b. anarchy, order, and constraints
    c. war, revolution, and famine
    d. the military, intellectuals, and bureaucrats

14. Globalists view international relations:
    a. from a historical perspective
    b. as taking place within a world capitalist system
    c. in terms of dependency relations
    d. all of the above

15. IGOs are:
    a. transnational organizations which bypass government
    b. multinational corporations
    c. voluntary associations of foreign states
    d. national liberation and terrorist groups

ANSWERS TO FILL IN THE BLANKS

A. 1. Act, attain their goals, interact
    2. 38, one-half billion
    3. similar
    4. regional cooperation
    5. 15, Russia
    6. world power, democracy, capitalism
    7. Slavic, Asian, Islamic
    8. petroleum
    9. Islam
    10. Japan, India, China
    11. Taiwan, Singapore, South Korea (and/or Malaysia)
    12. China, India

13. Sub-Saharan Africa
14. poorest, life expectancy, low
15. Anglo America, Canada, the U.S.
16. Resources, population, stability
17. Latin America
18. Spanish, Roman Catholic
19. Democratization
20. Rich, poor, instability

B. 1. international relations
2. conclusions
3. power, military strength
4. capacity, affect
5. national independence, honor, and well-being
6. competitive, absolute, diffuse, action-oriented, dynamic

C. 1. individuals, psychological factors, specific conditions
2. general, administrative, crisis
3. democratic ideology
4. isolationist, interventionist, internationalist

D. 1. values, roles, instruments
2. United Nations, foreign aid, collective security
3. governments
4. dependable
5. stretch

E. 1. relative
2. diplomacy
3. limited, differences
4. shifting alliances
5. become stronger
6. multipolar, bipolar

ANSWERS TO MULTIPLE CHOICE QUESTIONS:

1. c
2. d
3. d
4. c
5. a
6. c
7. c
8. d

9. b
10. d
11. e
12. b
13. b
14. d
15. c

NOTES

NOTES

NOTES

NOTES

NOTES

NOTES

NOTES

NOTES

NOTES

NOTES